Not Yet Post-Colonial:

Essays on Ghetto Being, Cosmology and Space in Post-Imperial Zimbabwe

Zvikomborero Kapuya

Edited by Tendai Rinos Mwanaka

Mwanaka Media and Publishing Pvt Ltd,
Chitungwiza Zimbabwe

*

Creativity, Wisdom and Beauty

i

Publisher: Mmap
Mwanaka Media and Publishing Pvt Ltd
24 Svosve Road, Zengeza 1
Chitungwiza Zimbabwe
mwanaka@yahoo.com
www.africanbookscollective.com/publishers/mwanaka-media-and-
publishing
https://facebook.com/MwanakaMediaAndPublishing/

Distributed in and outside N. America by African Books Collective
orders@africanbookscollective.com
www.africanbookscollective.com

ISBN: 978-1-77929-599-6
EAN: 9781779295996

©Zvikomborero Kapuya 2020

DISCLAIMER
All views expressed in this publication are those of the author and do not
necessarily reflect the views of *Mmap*.

iii

Acknowledgement

Foremost, I would like to acknowledge God, as the existentiality superior being who controls the society from the terrestrial world. I would like to extend my gratitude to my Parents, and family, and also mostly Dr P Mavhunga and family for their unwavering support in my interest in literature, governance architecture and decolonial thinking. My special acknowledgement also goes to Sharon Rutendo for her support, motivation and being a pillar of strength in writing this book. I would like to mention my academic mentor Dr A Chilunjika, illustrious public governance thinker for his laborious support in my academic journey. To my friends, workmates in the Department of Politics and Public Management, also my gratitude to Vengesayi architects for support with technical resources.

Dedication

Dedicated to Sharon Rutendo Ruswa, the late Professor John Mbiti and to all 'ghetto youths'

Table of Contents

Chapter 1: Not Yet Post-Colonial and Ghetto Consciousness: Shelling the Nut..1

Chapter 2: Historiography of Ghetto Culture in Zimbabwe..........25

Chapter 3: Reflection of Ghetto and Cosmology.....................35

Chapter 4: Image of Post-Colonial Ghetto Renaissance..............46

Chapter 5: Reimagining the Post-Colonial Ghetto Being in Zimbabwe: Soliciting Football.......................................56

Chapter 6: The Soul of Ghetto Space in Mbare.....................65

Chapter 7: Pentecostal Myth: The Soul of Ghetto Being...80

Chapter 8: Streets of Revolution: Rethinking woman in Ghetto Public Space...91

Chapter 9: Music in Post-colonial Ghetto: Winky D Decolonial Thoughts in Njema Songs..103

Chapter 10: The Betrayal to Post-colonial Ghetto Cosmology: Crimes, Identity Crisis and Self-hate.................................119

Chapter 11: Beyond Ghetto Culture: A Decolonial Project in Post-Humanistic Globe..131

Chapter 12: Epistle to Ghetto: Post-Scriptum in Thoughts in Search of Uhuru naUmoja...141

References...148

Mmap Nonfiction and Academic books...........................156

Preface

From my previous work, titled Phenomenology of Decolonizing the University: Essays of contemporary Thoughts in Africology, I provided material arguments, and diagnosed the social problem sourced from colonial curriculum and coloniality. I argued that, transplant curriculum and the complex coloniality of epistemology based on knowledge monopoly of the Western world is the reason why Africans lost self and become the other. I then proposed a decolonial design prescribed in Afrocentric perspective, which is open to interact with other centric views to understand different social cosmologies towards humanist society. This book, is a continuation of decoloniality project, whereby my passion for a better society extends to the shores of social-political issues such as ghetto being, space and cosmology. The language is much more philosophical to create a foundational primary knowledge in the existing debate of post-coloniality and the studies of subalterns, which Spivak (2010) once asked, Can Subaltern Speak? I stand as a spokesperson of the subalterns, but this time my focus was on ghetto being. I read much on Husserl work which attests the relationship of the body and the mind as well as relationship of being with objects and others in social space. Jacques Husserl and Martin Heidegger work are much more similar, since they describe the issue of being in itself and being for itself as consciousness. Ghetto being for itself resulted in the indoctrinated ideas from the environment which constitutes cognitive views of the society, relate to being for itself which is based on the liberation of the body and relations with others. It is arguably that, these philosophies are Eurocentric but one of the prominent clinical psychologist Chabani Manganyi develops the discourse of black existentiality. In his monograph "Being-Black in the World" in 1974, I used a number of his argument to construct the theory of ghetto being and ghetto cosmology in relation to establishing a genuine post-colonial society. I agree with Chabani Manganyi on the following, the detribalisation of blacks in urban areas, the creation of urban areas as labour reservoir, the loss of self-image, the policy of separate development and black consciousness as response to the apartheid-racist colonial policies, but I extends beyond the post-independence which I broaden the concept as response to coloniality and afro-fascist political repressions which resulted from the abortion of anti-colonial projects. Mahmood Mandani provides a critical analysis as the foundational thought of ghetto being and cosmology, and contributes to it largely in his book "Citizen and the Subject: The Legacy of Late Colonialism" which alienated and detribalise Africans. I discussed various issues in this collection of essays, and write it in the capacity of political science but it is worth to everyone who has interest in contemporary issues, ghetto being and also those who need to develop alternatives in searching self. Issues such as football, Pentecostalism, woman liberation and dancehall music are discussed in relation to ghetto space and being as themed by the reflective experiences in the contemporary social realities. I am deeply saddened with the continuity of self-hate, identity crisis and mental confusion which is celebrated as modern life and abort the mission towards a post-colonial state, I then propose a decolonial framework as only a solution to solve present challenges. Ghetto cosmology created in the objective of revolution against social injustice, and ghetto being is a revolutionary being, hence resources and framework is there to begin the journey, it is my hope to see Afrocentric consciousness consume the celebrated modernity in the search of post-colonial state. A decolonial paradigm, is not just an intellectual material but a strategy to map the way forward of total liberation and reclaiming the full humanity. Ghetto cosmology is not much different from Harlem renaissance since it is based on literary development, political consciousness and theatrical development as movement to confront the unjust world. This book, the engagements also profess to the futuristic politics of Cultural Revolution led by the marginalised people, woman and ghetto being, to fight for their rights and establish a true post-colonial society.

Zvikomborero Kapuya

Chapter One
Not Yet Post-Colonial and Ghetto Consciousness: Shelling the Nut

The tragedy with Africa is that, it is a creation and invention, following the words of Mudimbe (1988 and 1994). Its institutions such as universities, schools, parliaments and political institutions are created by the colonial governance, and did they end at the collapse of colonialism? An important question in this collection of essays- searching Africa in the map of post-colonialism- it is arguably that not only political and juridical institutions are created, but also epistemologies, languages, cultures, history and images are also created at the same time. Created by who? Africa once a great continent, approached the dark ages resultant from Arab conquest of kemet, Greeco-Roman imperialism, transatlantic slave trade and colonialism- which explains the combination of the Arabs and Caucasians in the creation of Africa today. But Mazrui (1986) broadcasting a documentary on BBC argued that, slavery was a profiting culture to the capitalist and dehumanised Africa, but it came to end, that colonialism surfaced as formidable culture and continued to dehumanise the global south, exploiting resources but it came to an end, is it for real? Of course as an event it reached its terminus at the collapse of apartheid in South Africa 1994, but coloniality continued and problematizes the existence of a 'post-colonial state'. The discourse "without" which was evangelised by the west to legitimise the creation of Africa, refered to people without historical conscience, people without a soul, people without development. So to fill all those empty spaces, an outsider came and claimed to fill that gap, which is absolutely

1

untrue, since Cheikh Anta Dip and a team of Afrocentric historians prove Africa's glorious past was a credit to all global civilisations. The continuity of colonialism, ceased to be an event but a system also existed in the global space which created confusions to newly independent states, for instance the genocide in Rwanda 1994, and civil wars in Democratic Republic of Congo and military coups in West Africa evidences the toxic magnitude of global coloniality. Zimbabwe tried to make herself a post-colonial state, embrace the political blueprints of pre-colonial state through land reform programme, titled third Chimurenga as continuing honouring Murenga Sororenzou and the past ancestry. Murenga Sororenzou was a priest in the past Shona societies, and 'Chimurenga' as war of liberation struggle was named after him, depicts the appreciation of cultures and past glory. The attempt threatens the goal power structures, and resulted into serious punishment through economic sanctions. All these efforts challenged by the existing mental confusions caused by the colonised curriculum (Mavhunga 2006), coloniality of epistemology in universities and public institutions, apart from this Afro-fascism rise into prominence as the manifestation of coloniality of being, identity crisis and self-hate which justifies the non-existence of the country in the map of post-coloniality. The situation in contemporary Zimbabwe, which described as ghetto condition disqualifies the post-colonial appeal of the state, the national building has been consumed by the flames of autocracy, neo-colonialism and the matrix coloniality. In this regard, a post-colonial state described by numerous authors such as Ndhlovu-Gatsheni, Ramon Grosfoguel, Giyatri Spivak, Achilles Mbembe, Paul Tiyambe Zeleza, Ali Mazrui and Lwazi Lushaba just to mention a few; their descriptions were based on Marxist social interpretation

2

which talk about social equality, decoloniality of knowledges, rethink cultures and literary narratives. These scholars are remembered and acknowledged in this collection of essays, but here a post-colonial state image is based on the existence of political liberties, reclamation of Ubuntu cultural cosmology for present and future blueprints in the dynamic world, Afrocentric modes of thinking, analysis and epistemology, free from Afro-fascism and reclamation of self-confidence. Ghetto cosmology originated in colonial ghettos to challenge the colonial brutalities, now it did not cease its objective of liberation; it continues in the post-imperial Zimbabwe, to confront the unjust world, reclaiming the lost ontologies and establish a genuine post-colonial state. The objective of this collection of essays is (1) to explore the existence of coloniality in the supposedly free African ghetto, Zimbabwe in particular, (2) it is also aimed at relating ghetto being, space and cosmology towards liberation project in recreating a genuine post-colonial society, (3) it aimed to explore the reflections of ghetto environment, activities and spaces which shapes behaviours of ghetto being, (4) exploring the challenges towards the creation of ghetto being and (5) provides decolonial alternatives to ghetto being's struggles for post-colonial existence in Zimbabwe and beyond.

The Existentiality of Ghetto Being: A Philosophical Image

The studies of experience and existence gain once a prominent discourse in philosophy, psychology, sociology, art and political science of the 20th century has now been overtaken by the philosophy of technology. The 21st century society is more engrained in technology, though patches of phenomenology are still there but the centrality of technology in human projects is more studied in the present century. Technology is now regarded as the pertinent issue in solving human problems due to its efforts in bringing the world closer, bringing New York closer to Harare which is defined as global village. It is a celebrated norm since it professes the 'civilised society' from the writings of Fredrich Hegel. Its impacts become too rosy to forget, since it centralises human problems and human beings in an attempt to solve human problems, but it did not totally substitute the prominent studies of phenomenology, since technology facilitates the movement of information and creation of new forms of knowledge. Human experiences in post-global world contributed immensely to the creation of social world, from nominalist point of view, labels and concepts defines social reality, human existence as constructed by human beings. The critical reflections of post-modern world, though machination substitutes human labour, humans are still at the centre of discussion and the decision of world; humans are still at the centre of every discussion and the decision of the world affairs. Fredrich Hegel and Martin Heidegger, defines being as in two folds, 'being for itself and being in itself which necessarily defines the scope of human consciousness and ability to tame, influence the environment. Consciousness is not just an in-built, but primarily influenced by the environment, sub-consciousness. Segmund Freud clarifies the relationship between environment and its relations to thinking being. Being for itself, gives credit to phenomenologist in the sense that, the output of consciousness to the principle which confirms John Locke psychological thought of human beings as born 'tabula rasa' (empty slate), as object. The kind of information being fed in humans' empty slate at pedagogy matters most in understanding the issue of existentiality. Education, society and media fed humans' empty slate, for instance, racism can intellectual be projected as aided by knowledge deposited to the blacks as inferior being and whites as superior beings which manifest in the behaviours of the two. As philosophical approach in modern political system, human beings are conditioned to think politically which informs the existentiality of being and in the studies of existence and experience, ghetto being is being unrecognised hence this project, mandated to develop the scope of 'being' relating to ghetto conditions. It is about human beings and environment, a source of identity and experiences. The main objective is to explore how ghetto experience, conditions and influences the existentiality of ghetto being, identity and culture. The triple analysis of the condition provides an adequate argumentation of how the impact by environment creates cultures and modes of cognitive behaviours. In the histories of post-colonial Africa, literature on urban culture did justice to define urban being, but failed to give a comprehensive thought on urban culture liberation. One of the forgotten clinical psychologists, Chabani Manganyi (1974) publishes an existential philosophy book on the existence of black modes of being in the world, titled "Being Black in the World' The sociological schema of blackness and cognitive discourses in apartheid environment. Being black in the world, introduces the book chapter on Urban Africans in South Africa, as the labour migrants, live in backyards of suburbs and ghettos in abject poverty, since their intellectual capabilities were relegated against that of European white descent, the main labour was physical and few could occupy mental related jobs and Africans were not allowed to join trade unions as a security threat to the existence of Apartheid. However, this situation creates a revolutionary being premised on the existence of cultural heritage, still exported to the urban areas by rural migrants and

5

hidden in the gourds of language. It is seemingly understood that, the first generation the colonial construct, ghettowized and forced into serious condition aims to erase humanness thinking among blacks in colonial society, though resisted unsuccessfully but the second generation plotted a new revolutionary system informed by history and cultural residues which even made industrial action and full-scale political movement. It proved that, ghetto colonial being were more political consciousness, though it adopted a European style of revolution which is Marxism as emancipatory ideology, in creating a non-racial society and classless society. This movement costed the revolution due to life imprisonments of leaders such ANC Nelson Mandela, PAC Mangaliso Sobukwe, detention of ZANU's Robert Mugabe, ZAPU's Joshua Nkomo and assassination of Amilcar Cabral, Hebert Chitepo, Steve Biko to mention a few. The revolutionary front created a political consciousness, emanated from brutal colonial experience to pursue freedoms of the body, spirit and soul. African ghetto experience is divided into two, colonial and post-colonial but informed by Africa's triple heritage which is explained in African tradition, Colonialism and Islam's Africa (Mazrui 1986), agree with Kwame Nkrumah Conciencism. The sad part of Africa is that Soweto in contemporary South Africa is still the same with apartheid era, the pre-independence Mbare in Zimbabwe is still the same with Mbare in present, not in infrastructure but in mentality, the mental slavery of ghetto being whereby abject poverty, denigration, violence, crimes, increases in divorces, drugs and breeding places for epidemic diseases. This condition, creates a different ghetto being who still has been cognitive, think of the power of revolution but fighting different systems, similar versions and some influenced by the older versions are still trapped in the snare. The post-colonial

6

ghetto being, its thinking is housed revolution against the residue of colonialism, political violence, limited freedoms, poor service delivery and marginalised youth. It is more assembled by the youth, responding to this deleterious situation hitting the surface of post-colonial politics. The imaginary construct of this philosophical analysis has been ignored, but matters most since some of the linguistic labels like "Madhiri" (deals), hwindi (bus agents), "Matsotsi" (deceivers) and 'ghetto youth'' premised on the concept of 'deconstructionism' and survival strategy in the supposedly free, independent and economically developed state. In this regard, the memories of revolutionaries such as Joshua Nkomo steers revolutions in Bulawayo, memories of Nehanda influences art, literature and poetry responding to the primary objective of Chimurenga and the contemporary political crisis and in South Africa Steve Biko influences decolonial movement, sloganize decolonization of the mind since it has been projected by the white epistemology to promote 'epistemicide' of native epistemology. In analysis, ghetto as European in making, its institutions are challenged to develop an Afrocentric project to channel the energy of revolution in developing a genuine post-colonial society, disassociate itself from complex coloniality. This book is about critical analysis discourse of ghetto experiences in ghetto being to define the existence of Zimbabwe in post-colonial era, contemporarily in the map of post-imperial which is not clearly seen due to trapped ghetto being. Ghetto being is the reflection of the constructed mode of thinking in responding to colonialism, coloniality and embracing the pre-colonial political blueprints in liberating the continent.

Theoretical Propositions of Ghetto Being

1) Post-Structuralism Analytics

Ghetto being and culture as theoretical discourse, this epistemic discourse does not hold immunity from social relations theory for a systematic argument and thought. Post-structuralist, though crippled in international relations, is also confirmed social relations and intellectual project themed at analysing human-social relations in a social world. Ghetto as part of the social world, the discourse of ghetto being has been literary developed as a new form of phenomenology of post-humanistic world, this is made possible by structural analysis of post-structural theory. The theory, reduced to a method of thinking, an intellectual project and analytics clarifies the evidence of the symbolic strength of European cultures, structures and the notion of responses. Post-structuralism developed by Michael Foucault, Judith Butler, Levi Strauss to mention a few, arguing that, the existence of meta-narratives and universal structures act in contrary to human project of freedom. For instance, the universal narratives of European superiority relegates the cultural growth of non-European beings around the world, which specifically argued that a Eurocentric method of meanings has been centred to modernity as progressive ideology. In ghetto construct, the main message or narratives communicates the idea of Euro-American superiority as intellectual, Literary and imaginary projects to demonize the other (Lezra 2010). Post-structuralist holds that, the relationship between self and the other maintained by hierarchy relations, which problematize the prevalence of meaningful multicultural society, whereby Europe self-remains superior to other (third world countries). This structure ambiguously limits the projects of civilisation, bifurcates the society on the superior and inferior

8

proliferated by education and social conditions to control human beings transcended to the ghetto being. In doing so, post-structuralist provides solutions, deconstruction of the existing structure credited by Jacques Derrida as worthy methodology of human literation from beings subjected by the social structures (Butler 2012). The theory exposes the propositional production of ghetto being epistemology since it's about deconstructing colonial structures such as labour, repressive laws as well post-colonial repressive political structures. Moving from post-structuralist theory to post-structuralist analytics creates credit to the development of ghetto epistemology, since it aims at explaining the cause, the systems and deconstruction systems as post positivist way of thought.

2. Historical Materialism Analytics

Historical materialism is a purveyor of all sorts of analysis of capitalist space as source of inequality and invites revolution to create an egalitarian society. It is by no doubt that, Russian Revolution theatricalising Marxism as source of political recourse, revolution and established governance. The leader of Russian Revolution, Vladimir Lenin transacts it from Marxist political theory and transform it into practical system. Russian Revolution, Chinese Revolution and decolonization movement, all supports the applicability of historical materialism. Though at the collapse of Berlin Wall is used to be the symbol of socialism and the fall of giant Union Soviet Socialist Republic (USSR) (Magstadt 2010, Fukuyama 1992) marks the death of the ideology, but it was not explained well, the interpretive discourse of socialism was not primarily attached to Berlin Wall as a symbol but Beijing, Accra and African countries still holds the policies of the ideology. In the context of ghetto, historical materialism analytics contributes to the intellectual development of ghetto being and culture, since industrial sociology, capitalism and socialism constructs the discourse. The theory founded by Karl Marx and Fredrich Engels address the increase of problems of poverty in industrial cities, whereby the rich become more rich and the poor become more poorer due to labour exploitation. Industrialist exploits labour from the proletariat, creates a class society, limits freedoms of the lower class since they were powerfully materially and control the state. In this regard, ghetto praxis in South Africa and colonial Rhodesia were structured in this colonial form, whites as industrial owners and blacks as proletariat, led to the development of value based on colour line, the dichotomy of black and bad, white and good since it strengthening the separatist racial policy. It disadvantages blacks more at work place. In dealing with such situation, revolutionary consciousness is aided through trade unions for collective bargaining and industrial actions. Of course they were trade unions in colonial past, but for whites and the question was who should join trade unions raised by the white unionist, fearing blacks nationalism possible rise from trade union and threatening the white government, but it did not stop revolutions; blacks increased in numbers as members of trade unions and organised strikes based on black consciousness, founded by Steve Biko as shared mutual knowledge of suffering aimed to liberate the existentiality of the black body, soul and the mind.

"The public marriage of the words 'black' and 'consciousness' has in some panic and public consternation in certain sections of the South African public. There have been arguments,

10

debates and naggings. It all happens so quickly that some observers have even suggested that the bogey swartgevaar was suddenly becoming real. After this marriage it even became customary for some liberal bent to suggest that, black South Africans were now turning racialist" (Manganyi 1973;17)

The contestations and debates of black consciousness which later led to the Soweto massacre and the assassination of Steve Bantu Biko once prescribed a revolutionary act against capitalism as anointed by the oils of European racism. Though the movement was viewed as racialist, it defined blacks as symbols of suffering, hence the shared mutual knowledge of suffering spread across Soweto ghetto and South African liberationist project. The hopes of black consciousness extend to the core of individual physical life style, de-campaigns black as bad and sloganizes the beauty of blacks through the glory of African cultures. This conditions, still aid the theoretical sustainability of Marxism to freedom. Ghetto being is about seeking freedom, but freedom cannot be achieved in linguistic terms since society has conditions, but the human remains with the authority to decide on whether to follow the social conditions from the greater good of the community or not. Industrial actions in Zimbabwe initiated ghetto political discussions, since some of them were illegal, followed pure Marxist prescription of laws, social structures as the opium of oppression. Marxist analytics believe in mutual shared discourse, though have long originated from Ubuntu philosophy, Socratic theory, platonic communism and Egyptian Ma'at (Asante 2000). Ubuntu once destroyed, but Marxist form of socialism defines the need for creating a classless society, to include ghetto marginalised society in the benefit of national resources, establishing a tyranny of majority and social democracy. In analysis, the implication of historical materialism to the intellectual development of ghetto discourse, constructs a substantive thought, systematic approach and pragmatic discourses of epistemologies associated with this theory. The theory explains the social structures, systems, the objective of revolutions and the governance system.

3. Transmodenity Approach

To provide a determinant and diverse approach, Transmodenity in post-colonial studies is too tempting to forget, due to its rosy, brilliant petals of analysis of Europeanised ghetto conditions, dialogue (relation), communication, existentiality and being. It is critical criticism of the existing mother body theories and challenges the methodologies of social change, epistemology towards human freedoms and the definition of universe in multicultural perspectives. The theory originated from post-structural analysis of being, society and narratives from the writings of Jürgen Habermas, Marx Hoikehimer and Theodor Ardono and goes beyond post-modern and Marxist methodology of human liberation, to self and society liberation. Post-modernism aimed at deconstructing the existing social and political designs, but Transmodenity take a further step, since the prescriptive thoughts suggests deconstruction alternatives but failed a comprehensive method, and in most cases the theory is criticised for being Eurocentric. Boarder Thinking (Anzaldua 1983), delinking (Amin 2009) and decoloniality (Mignolo 2013) shape Transmodenity methodological approach in dismantling the existing global coloniality in power, thought-power and being. The theory defines the world, as the Eurocentric construct, normative order sourced from Euro-American zones. The metaphysical existence is informed by the presence of the west history of civilisation and philosophy which today is now defined as coloniality (Quinjano 2000). Sylvia Wynter (2010), Dussel (1979), Anzaldua (1983), Grosfoguel (2007), Mignolo (2013) and Maldonado-Toress (2018) analyse the scope of coloniality, as the conditions that dehumanize, depersonalise, epistemicides non-western world, whereby it was facilitated through religion, trade, politics and education. But the main vehicle used is epistemology, Cartesian theory of knowledge enveloped in the mantle of culture and education, relegating knowledge of non-European beings, and creating coloniality of being, reduced to objects and subjects of western modes of thinking. Ndhlovu-Gatsheni (2015) explains how this metaphysical world is designed

Paradigm of Discovery and Mercantilist Order. This is evidenced by Christopher Columbus claims of the discovery of America and Africa. Discovery meaning to say an terra nullius (unihabitated lands) which accentuates Spain and Portugal colonial ambitions in today's Latin America, sustained by slave trade since the Valladolid Judgement refer to Africans as people without soul, hence legitimise transatlantic slavery

Post-1648 Westphalian Order. The creation of sovereignty states after the protracted thirty years war in Europe between Catholics and Protestants become the European political norms and superiority project continue to universalise Europe. This sovereignty projects exported to Africa through colonialism and proved to unfit to African ethnic confederacy states which today breeds lethal phobias and civil wars (Mazrui 1986)

1884-5 Berlin Conference. Premised on the scramble and partition of Africa, European countries discussed the future of Africa in her absence, share the portions of lands. This continued to construct Eurocentric projects of superiority and dehumanize since that is when the development of Africa's underdevelopment takes place (Rodney 1973)

Colonial governmentality (African subjectivity). Africans become subjects, ghettos created, and dehumanisation projects established to create the dichotomy of human beings and non-beings (Maldonado-Toress 2017), Apartheid South Africa was a good example of this social structure.

Post-1945 United Nations decolonisation normative order. The normative order continued the white supremacist project, African states were to exist at the bottom of the world civilisation, the dichotomy of developed and developing states creates global order of political hierarchy, whereby powerful states defined meaning of human rights in their cultural perspectives, created international laws and imposed the systems to the so called developing states

Post-Cold war triumphalism of neo-liberal Oder. This is to say, the collapse of socialism marks the victory of neoliberal Oder which favours democracy as political project, free trade and capitalism for economic development which disadvantaged the global south, and worked in favour of the western-capitalist states

Post-9/11 anti-terrorist Oder (new securitization). This era, gave much power of global governance to the west to invade countries in the name of anti-terrorism campaigns, demonstrating the existence of unjust world since those military campaigns meant to destabilise peaceful countries and loot resources in a chaotic environment.

Sabelo Ndhlovu-Gatsheni, a historian traces the genealogies of coloniality of power, being and knowledge in which the genetics is traced to the era of discoveries, however the historiographic construction sourced as far as the Greek philosophy, whereby it is sure that Greek philosophers stole Egyptian philosophy (George James 1954) and Fredrich Hegel philosophy of history also accentuated the existing of the norm. The discourse creates ghettos around the world, and help to redefine what actually means, by saying a ghetto being. The theoretical existence of coloniality of the images, soul, body and the mind by Euro-American systems caging non-Caucasians in ghetto so as to preserve the global hierarchy and normative order of white supremacism. From this global designs, it transcend the creation of labour settlements, which are later defined as ghettos or favelas. The living conditions there are embedded in dehumanization project. Coloniality of being manifest in violent self-hate and unethical beings proliferated by colonial institutions formulated on the foundation of coloniality of knowledge(s). Post-structuralist identifies these social conditions suggesting decolonial alternative as methodology for human liberation. Gloria Anzaldua (1983) goes beyond post-structural perspective in theorizing 'boarder thinking' as an alternative existence in the logical thinking responding to colonialism and its conditions. In this regard, ghetto political theatre was about the intense discussion of the condition of mutual suffering and suggest remembering the dismembered African values informing of intellectual criticism, demonstrations and industrial action against the systems that ghettowize them. The consciousness of freedom attempts to dismantle the colonial absurd situation, which drives Africans and non-European beings into ghetto condition. Mignolo (2000) also concurs that boarder thinking is the space where the restitution of subaltern knowledge, reorient with the past knowledges, medicinal secretes and heritage as source of energy to decolonial movement. Apart from boarder thinking, Amin (1980) introduces delinking as political redemptive strategy of delink the global south from the west, call for South-South cooperation to survive from the ferocious exploitative global coloniality. This situation creates a condition whereby the physical dislocation of the west and the other spare ghetto beings from coloniality of being manifest in self-hate and identity crisis. Ghetto beings and cultures calls for decolonised African states. In post-imperial projects, the issue of rewriting African past, decoloniality of epistemology and Afrocentric womanism remains the objectives of the revolutions in post-colonial ghettos. In understanding ghetto being, the history of colonialism as presented by the theory of Transmodenity provides a critical reflection of the rationale or ghetto urban settlements, and implications to ghetto being. This environment, creates a non-thinking being, but a revolutionary being aimed at not only deconstruct but decolonise ghetto space.

Scope and Organisation of the Book

This book is organised into several chapters, focuses on ghetto experiences and activities in relation to ghetto being manifest, in history of ghetto, ghetto being, Pentecostal myth, music, football and the metaphysical existence of ghetto as strategic urban settlements. The book is aimed at mapping the contours of new political thought based on defining human condition founded on the existentiality thought of ghetto being and cosmology in transcendental thought of the condition, being, space and system.

Though the book began at conceptualise ghetto being based on systematic philosophical approach, Chapter two breaks the historical grounds of the development of ghetto-urban settlements in colonial Rhodesia, resulted from colonialism, cultural alienation, detribalisation and industrial sociology towards emancipation. The chapter is aimed at providing a political project of colonial encounters of Africa and Europe, Europe as the master and cities such as Mbare begin to exist. The analogous analytics employed is to give a critical analysis of the discourse. The author concludes that, African cultures remain an oasis of ghetto liberation projects nourishing the objectives of rebellious activities against the European systems of colonial project. The chapter titled "Historiography of Ghetto Cosmology". From historical development, the need to define ghetto cosmology and being help the reader in the journey of comprehending this book project. Chapter three of the book titled "Reflection of Ghetto Being and Cosmology", theoretically analyse the position of these named concepts to cultivate the philosophical project in developing theory of dialogue, existentiality and being in ghetto and outside. As a culture originated from ghetto urban settlements, a revolutionary culture breaks walls of geographical locations to include rural and suburban youth spread through music and political conditions. Ghetto cultures formed to fight colonialism and political repression in post-colonial Zimbabwe, questioned as Afrocentric invention to support the argument with Transmodenity oppositions. Call for re-centre African agency in ghetto culture embraced as true liberation project. To be a ghetto youth does not mean to live in ghetto, but have a culture of deconstructing the source of ghetto conditions which is colonialism, coloniality and political repressions. Understanding ghetto culture, open the avenues of comprehending art and intellectual development as the imaginary construct of post-nationalistic Zimbabwe. Chapter four titled "Ghetto Renaissance in Post-colonial Zimbabwe", founded on Mudimbe (1994) political diagnosis of African tragedy, state that "the problem with Africa is that it is an invention", hence ghetto renaissance as replica of Harlem renaissance or aid Thabo Mbeki's African Renaissance recreates African art and poetry as to reclaim the continental ontology but premised on history of Africa in world politics. In solving the problem of intellectual vacuum originated from the content's Dark Age, the colonial era, the continuity of traditional music and the genesis of Afro-Jazz music in most popular remembered records performed by Hugh Masekela, Oliver Mutukudzi and Thomas Mapfumo evidence the existence of Afrocentric consciousness towards past, present and future of African ghetto conditions. Urban grooves and Zimdancehall dominates the post-colonial Zimbabwe entertainment space representing youth voices, speaking about the marginalisation of youth and other themes of social experiences. This chapter, largely reference Harlem Renaissance as point of reference of development of ghetto cosmology, speak about suffering through poetry and theatre congests ghetto societies, attracting numbers as revolutionary movement. The author expresses the vast knowledge of philosophy, in relating the environment with being, soul and the mind and communication structures through attitudinal discourses's search for freedom and liberation, not just from colonialism or coloniality but from fascist-nationalist regimes in post-colonial society. It is not just only literature or politics, what makes this book unique in relating ghetto social conditions of football to the development of ghetto consciousness through football not as a sport only but dominating ghetto space as a method to escape the realities of contemporary ghetto conditions. Chapter Five titled, "Reimagining Post-Colonial Ghetto Space and Being in Zimbabwe: Soliciting Football", explained the trajectory of ghetto consciousness through football, from streets football to domestic leagues but globalisation contributed immensely to football consciousness, globalised soccer has become a major social system, magnet with youth together for entertainment and breeds revolutionary consciousness. This is a splendid assemblage of thought, unites the issue of soccer as trending ghetto soul which simply confuses on why especially globalised football attract people in numbers, watched in bars, what solution to life does it provide? As a result of poor economic system, relates with mind, soul and body in search of happiness as utmost human desire to escape the realities of absurd social space. Mapping the contours of ghetto cosmology, the author confirms the development of ghetto being using case study in chapter six, the chapter titled "The Soul of Ghetto Being in Mbare". The mandate is to explain how ghetto residential areas are created, since Mbare is the oldest urban centre in Zimbabwe with historical legacy of colonialism. The historical development of urban centre in Salisbury bring memories of colonial past whereby Africans snatched their lands, detribalised and colonially subjugated. It brings the memories of colonial racial inequalities, industrial action in search of equality and political activism. In contemporary society, the city is now marred with poor service delivery resultant from corruption, as the market centre of the country characterised by the massive depletion of maintenance and service delivery whereby responsible authority failed to maintain the city due to corruption and incompetency of bureaucrats in City of Harare. Mbare is the market place and is characterised by the existence of technical entrepreneurship, but as a result of economic conditions, the city is too crowded and crime rate is at its peak. The ghetto being in revolutionary politics also shaped by the imminent rise of Movement of Democratic Change (MDC) and Government of National Unity (GNU), Mbare is the symbol of political contestations, independence and the historical legacy of colonialism. Chapter Seven of the book unspare the Pentecostal revolution in post-independence ghetto, as the factor shapes the image and thinking of a ghetto being. The Chapter titled "Pentecostal Myth or Reality: Ghetto Prophet", influenced to be inked resultant from the massive explosion of Pentecostal faith in Zimbabwe 21st century. The chapter aims to give an assumptive explanation of why now? Why not in colonial Zimbabwe, and analyse the narrative allegedly religious entrepreneurship, and the ordeal of exorcism as well miracles as source of hope in absurd economic environment. Though Pentecostal act as puritanical methodology of Christianity calling for the restoration of the true teaching of Jesus Christ, its gospel of prosperity raises eyebrows on its credibility. This situation shapes ghetto being, in most cases is also used as revolutionary society against the incumbent regimes accused of serious corrupt activities and gross violation of human rights. As popular culture, Pentecostal discourse is largely a ghetto, but to complete this liberation project the question of woman in public space scrutinised in chapter eight. What woman? Whose woman? Woman in whose public space? These questions formulates the argument of ghetto being on the question of woman, in defining woman biologically, culturally and socially and how they relate to the objects and space in ghetto. The chapter titled, "Streets of Revolution: Rethinking Woman in Ghetto Public Space", ghetto public space is patriarchal dominated since pre-independence

Zimbabwe whereby the revolutionary icons as products of ghetto are largely male. The space constructed in patriarchal structure due to protestant-catholic cultures, colonial politics and labour policies. However, the twining of social liberation with woman emancipation significantly open up public space for woman to participate actively in education and leadership, though liberal, Marxist feminism informing the political decisions on the question of woman in public space, the domain of Afrocentric heritage elevates the arguments of Afrocentric womanism as one of the key theoretical framework for the policies of social and dialogue relations. The chapter defines ghetto being, not only as man but balance the equation of woman and man towards the liberation project. The construction of ghetto being through non-sexist perspective sustains the post-colonial reasoning as embedded on past social blueprints where woman were once great generals, priest and queens in public spaces across Bantu cultures. Music and youth are indispensable, Zimdancehall entice the society, provides entertainment and the lost hope. One of the ghetto music icon Winky D cannot be forgotten in ghetto being analytic perspective, due to aid form to the culture inform of branding the new version of dancehall, which is Zimbabwean. Chapter nine titled "Muzik in Post-Colonial Ghetto Space: Winky D Decolonial Thoughts in Njema Song", it is noted that, every album launched by this music icon receive massive support in ghetto, hence the author analyse the normative discourse in it since the music touches all facets of life. However ghetto culture is a revolutionary, but the continuity of coloniality of being teamed up with barbaric-narcissist nature of human beings betrays the objective of the culture and manifest in form of self-hate, drug abuse and criminal activities. Chapter titled "The Betrayal to Ghetto Cosmology", youth composed ghetto being but the challenge is the increase in drug abuse swept away by the revolutionary objective, reducing it to a chorus of immoral songs. Fortunately Cress Welsing (1991) provides reflective thoughts of in comprehending this discourse, condemning it as a form of demeaning, self-hate as manifestation of mental slavery and coloniality of being. Transmodenity shapes the forms of knowledge of the discourse of 'ghetto being', relating to culture, environment and even exploring beyond the relationship of the mind (subject) and body (object) since the conditions formerly established by Europeans was using their cultures. Chapter ten provides a philosophical-pragmatic view on ghetto culture in decolonial perspective, since the project of creating the post-colonial Zimbabwe is well defined through decolonizing the idea of Zimbabwe, knowledges and post-independence cultural structures, the chapter titled "Ghetto Culture and Beyond: A Decolonial Project". It aims to give a template to decolonize ghetto being, space and activities for true liberation. The concluding chapter is an epistle; author presents a convictions, philosophies and message to the post-independence Zimbabwe, communicating the ideas beyond decoloniality, political repression and the importance of inclusivity-governance structure. The chapter titled, "Epistle to Ghetto: Postscriptum Thoughts in Search of Uhuru naUmoja".

Normative Analysis of Reflective Thoughts of Ghetto Modes of Being; A Post-Colonial Survey

The most astonishing fact in developing this discourse is based on analytical perspective of modes of being manifest in individualism and communitarianism. Social world exist not outside human cognitive as scientific realist claims, but human interaction nominal construct, hence whatever the structure of the society, it is not immune to human minds, actions and activities. For modes of being, the racial differences and universalisation of Imperial Being to other parts of material world confirms the development of the mind-set of individualism premised on the material context of the world (Manganyi 1973). Human beings are born selfish individual, that's what nature entails, but the normative order of the space has profound impact on the process of creating thinking images and modes. From Descartes point of view, "I think Therefore I am" unspare in logical analysis of this discourse, whereby in ghetto, Africans grab shovels to add the last soil to the grave of their own culture, buried it alive and replace it with individualistic culture, having greedy over material and property accumulation proposed by John Locke and evidenced in industrial revolution. Money economy profess greedy to ghetto culture, once referred by literature High Priest Dambudzo Marechera , "the world is sick, the disease is money", being a slave of it and the process of search for it executed in some deadly methods, ranging from exploitation, serious milking of the poor and cultism. At first of nationalism due to this individualism of mode of being the movement remain closed in the mantles of dreams since there was absence of social unity, people and culture were parallel which simply explains how social fabrics lost its relevance and also is the much needed issue to project post-colonial humanist projects. Chinua Achebe in 'Things Fall Apart", popularly explains how cultures has been murdered, his famous quotation states that "he has put knife on things that held us together, we have fallen apart", not fallen apart as individual but what makes the collective identity of Africa, raped, murdered and in some parts

23

buried alive by the colonialist. However, African cultures were once communitarian. Invested in people since sloganize on the banner of "I am because we are", the collective identity was not just a tale of formal system but the sacred bond which unites not just only bodies but souls and the minds of the people. It define what people are, Bantu philosophy (Wiredu 2002) has been a strong powerful norm which is sacred, go beyond spirit established by the worshiped highest being (God or Mwari) manifest in social complex practices. Though colonialism attempts to totally wipe it out, it failed to annihilate it totally by allowing rural society to exist, acting as the dwelling place of the survived cultures in languages and cultural practises, the mass rural-urban migration reunites the detribalised ethnic groups and reawakening the society towards revolutionary complex due to consciousness, a mutual knowledge based on shared suffering formerly creating the communitarian society again; people blended in the spirit of liberation. The re-affirmation of communitarian ghetto consciousness is a critical approach in modes of being which determines and portrays the image as the revolutionary strategy in nationalistic struggle. This also continues to post-colonial society, a ghetto beings portrays the communitarian thinking whereby abject poverty, political violence and the crisis of postcolonial state, further creates a communitarian, unfortunately this kind of society is not the same by the past conquering the present space to plan for the future, but it should not be immune to decoloniality, since this diagnosis of mutual confusion caused by coloniality is an evil situation prevailing, needs to be deconstructed, rather than decolonisation.

Chapter Two
Historiography of Ghetto Culture in Zimbabwe

Abstract

The historical narratives of colonialism provides critical materials in understanding the thought power of ghetto-colonial construction, the history of colonialism or the discourse of colonialism which is defined in the context of ideographic analysis, as an event came and end which was charactised by the colonial domination of the other (Africa, Asia and Latin) and the self-proclaimed global self (Europe). This paper is mandated to explore ghetto culture historically and question Zimbabwe social history from its singularity expression of history rather than 'histories', since the history of the ghetto is not treated as independent, but part of the history of political struggles which is amicable but have left out some important facts to be examined. Using political science Afro centeredness modes of analysis, the paper unpack the colonial metaphysis of the west, the exported values and how it has been indigenised and used as the method to realise and rise against the brutal oppression. Kwame Nkrumah political thoughts in Conciencism is not to be ignored, since it provides the philosophical framework of understanding how traditional cultures, Christian colonial cultures and Islamic culture define the model of African state of today and future. First Chimurenga, Black Nationalism and the creation of urban centres informs the analytic method of this study. It is believed that ghetto culture contemporarily is shaped by post-colonial political blueprints and the need to liberate ghetto being.

Key Words, Histories, Ghetto

Introduction

The synergy of Zimbabwe political history, informed by the pre-colonial power systems, Ndebele-Shona relations after Tshaka Zulu Mfecane dubbed Southern African war and the history of colonialism as an event and system. Ghetto cosmology and being invested in Marxist approach of revolution, to fight the ghetto conditions created by the colonial regime to serve the purpose of exploitation and dehumanization. Why ghetto cultures become so significant in the liberation of the marginalised Blacks? Harlem Renaissance, Soweto Uprisings, Haiti Revolution and Salisbury Industrial actions provides a critical comprehension on how the oppressed realise there are oppressed, and rationally decided to liberate their bodies, mind, soul and space. From its onset, ghetto as condition created to mummify African cultures, detribalise and collapse the sacred values of the people of the South. The main thrust of this paper is to explain the historical dynamics of ghetto culture, urban development and the role of industrial sociology in defining the historical context of 'ghetto being space and culture'. The reaction against oppression conceives popular struggles against the capitalist, influenced by the intense political discussion in ghetto space. The history of ghetto culture also illuminates the presents of bifurcated society, low density and high density suburb as confirms the existence of class struggles in the country's political system, explored into full scale war from 1966-1979. Although the war was on land issue (Muchemwa 2013), but the issue of labour exploitation and residential struggle also play a crucial

26

role to the existence of war of liberation struggle in Zimbabwe history.

Collapse of African Ontologies: A Historical Analysis of Urban Culture

Lezra (2010) conceptualise the discourse of demonization of the other. The relationship of 'self' (Europe) and the other (colonies) in terms of cultural development, whereby cultures of the other demonized, decrypted and was replaced with the so called civilised culture from the West. That's why colonialism justifies as mission civilistrice, where urban culture is a part of social domination was a component of the crusades of civilising the other. Post-structuralism provides a philosophical position of the 'other' and self, whereby Butler (1990), Derrida (1994) and Foucault (1980) teamed up to define the social structures challenging human freedoms, since the self (Europe) interacts with the 'Other' (colonies), the relations hierarchized, that's how White supremacism constructed. In this regard, racism born out for sustaining the Western universe in global system as imperial ideology, demonizing of the 'other' ghettowize Africans, reduce them into non-humans, dames (Fanon 1967) and impose the European way of thinking (Dusell 1973, Anzaldua 1983, Ndhlovi-Gatsheni 2018). The central concept of demonizing African cultures is to remove possible threat from social unity embedded in cultures, a threat to European existence in Africa. Said (2003) theorise the idea of global sociology in the context of "Occident" and "Orients', whereby orients (third world) referred to non-beings, inferior to the Occident's (west), this global set up rooted in Hegel philosophy of history, whereby historically conscious people qualified

27

to be human beings, and those who lack historical conscience or people without history were subject to be marginalised, exploited since there are not humans enough (Maldonado-Torres 2016). This structure, justifies Lezra (2010) hypothesis of the other as object, to be subjected and demonized, denied humanity, marginalised to the periphery and referred to as people without senses, clearly shows the implementation of demonization as structural imperialist ideology.

> "We went from the sixteenth century characterisation of people without history, from seventeenth century of people without writing, to twentieth century people without development, to 21st century characterisation of people without democracy" (Grosfoguel 2007)

The concept 'without' related to the metaphysical existence of Africa and its ontological existence created deliberately to justify the European domination as the method to fill that emptiness. The discourse 'without' did not spare African cultures from exotic domination, already declared weak, barbaric, which technically means dead, in presence of a political system the people of the south referred to as a people without 'technology'. This discourse constructs the ever ending inferiority of the global south and fund Euro American purgatory project to annihilate cultures of the colonies (Grosfoguel 2008, Quinjano 2000).

Nelson Maldonado-Torres, a leading scholar in decoloniality, summarise the discourse of the construction of the 'other', based on coloniality of power, thoughts and being. The universalisation of Imperial being in the global south imposes an extraordinary threat to the ontological existence of non-European being, threatens aesthetics and the way of thinking which popularise the opposing African epistemology premised on the communitarian template manifest in the phrase states that, "I am because we are" with Rene Descartes philosophy "I think, therefore I am" based on individuation mode of being (Maldonado-Torres 2016). In this regard, Africans are historically produced.

> "Key argument is that the Africa is not only a social and political construction but also a victim of imposed identities and this reality has made African political trajectories to continue to progress into ceaseless direction of struggling to negotiate themselves above existentially imposed singularities as part of resisting the reality of being 'fenced' in by the particular identity markers which they have not chosen themselves (Ndhlovi-Gatsheni 2013).

Africa as a political construct, which Mudimbe (1991) argued that the problem with Africa is that it is an invention, hence this led to current political turmoil, shown a ceaseless directions. Contextualising the discourse of ghetto creation in the prism of coloniality, colonialism dehumanizing Africans after Anglo-Ndebele war and First Chimurenga 1986, urban culture was exported by Europe to colonies. This is not a history to forget, though it is constructed through Eurocentric Designs, but it creates a new wave of indigenous thinking themed at implementing social revolution to confront the unjust world, both in cognitive and material world. The death of Africanity in the urban culture, offloads English culture, reduces black bodies into objects, with empty souls functioning as a result of imposed thoughts, non-thinking beings rather than subjects functioning on their own volition (Dibash 2013). The demand in commercial and industrial labour creates farm compound, mining urban areas and ghetto residential suburbs. Mine towns such as Gatooma, Kwekwe, Shabanie and Shurugwi were formed as labour repositories to nearby mines. In Salisbury, Highfields and Mbare were established as residential areas to supply labour to nearby industrial areas in Southerton. In this regard, due to policy of separate development it created a space for political discussions, news of Ghana Independence 1957 also influences political debate. The reserve system also led to the influx migration of natives from rural areas to urban areas in search for employment which congests the city, but though detribalisation successively implemented but these migrants came with rural cultures on medicines, customs especially Nyasaland immigrants. For Mandani (2010), the creation of bifurcated society based on citizen (urbanites) and subjects (rural folks) successfully collapse African kinship, community cosmology and the way of governance. African laws replaced by Roman-Dutch laws, customs replaced by the idea of modernity (Mignolo 2013). The collapse of African cosmology, cherishes coloniality of being, stripped Africans to naked and breeds social pathologies.

Theatre of Political Discussions; Historical Materialism

The relationship between the other and self, inferior and superior, black and white construct an ugly social phenomenon, breeds a rare kind of violence and positively the idea of emancipation. For the first time, the recognition of racial equality composed in Pan Africanism political ideology influences the increase in political discussions in beerhalls and public sphere (Ranger 1980, Mahomva 2014,

Mahomva, Chigora and Lunga 2019). The realisation of freedoms, founded on the history of pre-colonial society, influences intellectual discussions about governance, freedom, black question and land question. The emerging intellectual groups in ghetto won the arguments, since some were pessimistic about the issue of black rule, viewed it as biblical allusion, since Malcom X divides Negroes in two. House Negros and Field Negro, whereby the former is more reluctant to change, benefits from the system while the later experience harsh living experiences, in doing so House Negroes were foreman's, bass boy in suburbs, thinking the situation is right and cannot be changed (Woodson 1933). The story of Ghana Independence and Pan Africanism projects install hope on better view on black government on pluralistic society free from racial prejudices. Pan Africanism assumes a political, economic, intellectual and social consciousness build on aspirations of promoting liberty and global synergies of Africans in face of deliberate imperial marginalisation (Mahomva 2014). Zeleza (2007) defines it as Black Nationalism aimed to liberate Africans in Africa and Africans descent in diaspora. From this scholarly definitions, Pan Africanism is a wholescale movement of Africans around the world aimed at liberating them from all forms of social injustices founded on Trans-Atlantic slave trade, colonialism and neo-colonialism. The ideology influenced by revolutionary movements such as colonial resistance in Zimbabwe 1896. These historic events of colonial resistance and past glory (Sertima 2002, James 1954, Clarke 1998, Marimba Ani 1994 and Ben Joachanan 2000) creates a consciousness of black superiority (Diop 1974) and stages a revolutionary ideology to connect Africans with the past glory. Political discussions in the ghetto of Harlem provides practical resolution, since Marcus Garvey call for 'back to

Africa dream' which led to the creation of Liberia, freed slaves migrate from USA to trace the roots in Africa. W.E.B DuBois and Gorge Padmore call for intellectual discourse in the construction of emancipatory projects of the people of colour. The discussions at Harlem Renaissance utterly kick start the movement, whereby Edward Blyden develop thoughts of African personality, Leopold Senghor the Negritude, Steve Biko Black Consciousness and George Padmore African socialism to explain the determinates and philosophical convictions of Pan Africanism. Kwame Nkrumah, Jomo Kenyatta, Julius Nyerere, Modibo Keita and Patrice Emery Lumumba from African ghettos emerge as revolutionary figure, pragmatism as the idea of African nationalism which conceive Ghana in 1957 and the Organisation of African Unity in 1963. In this regard, Pan African assemblage and contestation of ideas sustained the intellectual discussions by the marginalised in Ghetto areas. Pan Africanism as the centre of discussion, Smith regime cross-examined, questioned and de-legitimised in the lances of Africanity which communicates a political action to be orchestrated. Marxist ideology, as Afro-Marxist originated from socialist manifesto by Karl Marx, describe the condition of social inequality prescribed in 'have and have not' as a result of the exploitation. The method to rebut exploitation inequality and social injustices is to create ideal society, through unionism and revolution, hence Afro-Marxist ideology spread quickly in ghetto political discussions (Ranger 1985). Similar to Harlem Renaissance in USA Ghetto, ghetto voices entrenches the idea of socialist politics, culturalise revolution as emancipatory ideology. However, the idea of liberation and liberties spread from ghetto to rural areas, whereby ghetto-reserves interface creates a strong revolution forces with understanding of liberties and merge it with African cultures for unity.

Industrial Sociology and Demand for Political Space

The increase in brutalisation, racism, exploitation and denial of political freedom by the Smith regime invited popular uprisings on the marginalised demanding social justice and an end to selective application of policies and laws. The social condition, as the continuation of dehumanization of African beings, even in Soweto South Africa understood by blacks, trade unions and directed their anger to the Smith government. Low wages, poor working conditions and racism in Industrial relations challenged by the workers. Benjamin Burombo, Joshua Nkomo, Ndbanhingi Sithole and R.G. Mugabe as ghetto residents and workers organises industrial actions demanding better wages and non-exploitation working conditions (Bhebhe 1989). The struggle continues, not only as labour movement but demand political space in the slogan of 'one man one vote' (Ranger 1985). As influenced by Marxist Ideology, trade unions transformed into political parties fighting political injustices. Bantu Voters Association, African National Council (ANC), National Democratic Party (NDP), Zimbabwe Africa People's Union (ZAPU) and Zimbabwe Africa's National Union (ZANU), these political parties search for political space invites large followers from ghetto though being brutalised by Smith's Regime under the provision of Law and Order Maintenance Act (LOMA). However, the urban Marxist ideology's search for equality and an end to exploitation, transferred to the issue of means of reduction in rural areas, and mobilised support and engagement in guerrilla warfare since the

33

majority of foot soldiers were from rural areas, and leadership from the ghetto. Reserves-ghetto interface marks the beginning of new forms of consciousness to reunite Africans as a collective group to fight the common enemy. The once deprived African values, remembered in urban-rural interface solidifies the movement against colonialism.

Conclusion

Waiting for the Rain, a Charles Mungoshi writing about the setting sun of colonialism whereby the hopeless ghetto were sparked with ecstasy and euphoria for Independence. Marshall Munhumumwe, Thomas Mapfumo, Oliver Mutukudzi and Simon Chopper Chimbetu among others, nourishes happiness to the crowd, those in ghetto and rural areas celebrating the dawn of new era. Ghetto becomes the haven of intellectual development and political discussion. As this paper alludes, the historiography of ghettoism is too tempting to ignore, its relations with coloniality of being, political struggle and nationalism is applauded. However the answer remains, on the Afrocentric nature of ghetto culture?

Chapter Three
Reflection of Ghetto Being and Cosmology

Abstract

What is ghetto cosmology? Whose ghetto? Is ghetto a Nation? The growing trends of new ontology in post-colonial Africa has influenced the history of colonialism, liberation struggle and traditionalism as confirmed by Kwame Nkrumah Philosophy is Conciencism, shapes the post-colonial ghetto space, being and the development of key ontology which is not mere cultures, but exists a liberationist cosmologies. Ghetto culture, a new social phenomenon develops an indigenous system, a revolutionary act to maintain the sovereignty and challenge the existing status quo marginalising youth. The post-humanistic agenda, though cannibalistic in Nietzsche philosophy, but at local discourse is 'albeit fenced in political unit', informs the more humanistic ways to complete revolution. These questions informs the philosophical ideation of the study, whereby ghetto is no longer a shanty settlement, but settlement strategy act as condition to led to the formation of ghetto culture. It goes beyond municipality demarcation, but now is a culture in the hearts of youth, a revolutionary act aimed at demanding political-space using different methodologies.

Key Words: Ghetto Being, Ghetto Nation
Introduction

The main thrust of his paper is to define ghetto cosmology and ghetto culture in conceptual discourses founded on post-structuralism and critical social theory. As confusing terms not yet defined, its relationship to post-humanistic nationalism is of profound importance in epistemology of the discourse. The phenomenology experience, histories and the construction of ghetto as a form of residential settlement influences nominal development of certain axioms which extends even in suburban areas and rural areas. Pre-independence Zimbabwe shows the massive role of African culture, but later revolutionaries and, hangs with rural cultures to defeat the imperial system. At the crossroads, new forms of ghetto, quite different from colonial Zimbabwe mainly congested by the 'born free' or unemployed graduates youths marks the massive turning point of the Zimbabwe post-Chimurenga culture. The Afro-centric discourse of ghetto cosmology is seen on the need to emancipate Africa, through home grown industries and indigenous movement developing an Afro-centred music to unite the so called 'ghetto youth". Focusing on ghetto as the lived space reflects a colonial history, ghetto cosmology's rise to prominence in post-colonial Zimbabwe; unfolds the new era of revolutionary politics based in understanding of human rights, democracy and literary renaissance.

Conceptual Discourse of Ghetto Cosmology

The creation of ghetto residential areas was at the same time dehumanization of the other (Lezra 2010, Maldonado-Torres 2018), whereby ghetto referred to the settlements of non-beings and were located in industrial fumes and noise areas. African urban areas were meant for labour reservoirs. In post-colonial Zimbabwe ghetto become most important residents, because of its historical legacy, symbol and a centre of activities though marred with poor service delivery (Makumbe 1998). For Sachikonye (2011), operation Murambatsvina were targeting MDC supporters living in ghetto, since population increases sends a signal to the incumbent regime about the end if its hey days, though there is magnitude of truth in Sachikonye (2011) analysis, the operation was meant to restore cleanliness, demolish illegal structure and restore cities' image. What if today, operation Murambatsvina did not take place, cities will be ugly? In doing so, ghetto cosmology in post-second Chimurenga culture is a structural phenomenon responding from ghetto condition, mainly fenced into political boundaries and beyond. As a social phenomenon, conditions act as the problems that led to the formation of ghetto culture in post-colonial episode as reminisce of 1950s politics. Youth are at the forefront denouncing social injustices and the structural system of governance structure. In South Africa, politicisation of public administration reaps or harvest poor service delivery which resulted in massive service delivery protests; these conditions creates social crisis in urban areas. In this regard, ghetto axioms are a social phenomenon, fighting social injustices in development, since ghetto areas are marred with poor service delivery but politicians, business tycoons and wealthy people resides in low density suburbs such as Glenlorne, Borrowdale and Mount Pleasant in Harare, receive better services, this kind of bifurcated society formulates the post-colonial objectives of ghetto culture not in is truest socialist sense but creating a well-defined equal society. It threatens the process of post-colonial national building, symbolising a capitalist society which was once fought against in second Chimurenga and also creates another form of Chimurenga for recreating a just society. The critical component of ghetto culture is consciousness of mutual shared knowledge of suffering and revolution as psychological response to the existing ghetto conditions. From post-structuralism point of view (Butler 1990, Foucault 1973), these ill-conditions were used as a method of social control, creating social classes, the dichotomy of superior-inferior as capitalist model of society, however responding from these conditions, a mental disorder approach is applied which in other instances is called revolution, it's a realisation of the need for freedom but using a method which is beyond reason to negotiate space (Fanon 1963). In the context of Zimbabwe, the increase in unemployment and economic crisis, ghetto culture is no longer geographical bound but it goes beyond rural areas and low density. It is now an ideology, a nation, an identity carried in the hearts of man and woman affected by the present conditions and politics. "We are ghetto youth", what it means, is its just an identity? This slogan, sometimes sound cliché but it carries loads of situations, culture and blueprints for existentiality. Being a ghetto youth means being conditioned in serious crisis, marginalised but optimistic towards social change. It is a revolutionary culture aimed at giving hope to the unemployed graduates and political victim. The most interesting part of a ghetto cosmology is that it is not patriarchal at the same time it is founded on Afrocentric epistemology, an epitome of Harlem Renaissance. Ghetto is now a nation, a culture premised on the principle of responding to socio-economic environment in the marginalised society and nourished by music as spiritual movements towards an optimistic youthful society. It reminisces of Harlem renaissance, and later breeds civil rights activist about black empowerment.

Ghetto Space and Youth Revolution: Sociological Reflections

Revolution remains a trusted methodology for social change, it might be military revolution which is exemplified by the Chinese Revolution and social revolution based on non-violence movements, the Ghandian non-violence movements is an example. French revolution, a popular political movement in 1789 whereby citizens revolted against the monarch and its oppressive nature since struggle the for liberty, fraternity and freedom advocated by philosophers, such as Voltaire, Rousseau and Montesquieu in the struggles for liberating the peasants from brutal class society. African revolution is influenced by Marxist ideology as a response to colonialism and is aimed at establishing Afro-socialist governments (Davidson 2013). In the context of ghetto culture, it is founded a century ago, as revolutionary aspect, fighting workers exploitation and colonialism. This system, though, achieved its aims in 1980, it continues as popular culture whereby ghetto streets become streets of revolution, fighting injustices. Bridges become rendezvous for ghetto youth in discussing the reflective situation of life and its relations to the political system, that's why ghetto youth are always on the forefront of every demonstration hoping to change the situation. Ghetto youth are the army, waiting to be unleashed, more energetic, united due to mutually shared knowledge to negotiate space. It is a culture as old as pre-independence Zimbabwe and also its objective is to continue revolution if the classes were not abolished. The relationship between ghetto culture and youth revolution bridges the gap of pre-independence and post-independence Zimbabwe, whereby ZANU and ZAPU attracted crowds from ghettos around the country during Smith regime, but today a new opposition political party attracts ghetto youth in large numbers hoping for change. The long hope created in colonial times haunt the present society; constructing a revolutionary agenda towards achieving the incomplete objectives.

Ghetto Ontology: An Afrocentric Invention?

Is African ontology still relevant? Ghetto society provides a critical reflection on new African culture, which Kwame Nkrumah terms Conciencism, built by the pre-colonial and colonial history of the continent. In this regard, African ontology from the writing of Nabudere (2013), Hauntodnji (1993) and Wiredu (2002) is based on reimaging the post-colonial Africa in the lenses of cultural heritage on the past, but informed by the present situation to create the Africaness future. Further analysis of the question, an Afrocentric point of view, provides a clear answer to the existentiality of African ontology in ghetto space. The question on the Afrocentric nature of ghetto culture forms the philosophical ideation of this paper, whether ghetto culture is Afrocentric or not, it challenges and constructs its emancipatory discourses. Ghetto created by the European imperialist for labour and dehumanization objectives, hence how can it be Afrocentric? If ghetto manages to destroy African kinship (Mandani 1993), ethnicity and cosmology embracing western modernity (Mignolo 2013), how then does it breeds new Afrocentric thinking? Afrocentric is a philosophical template and paradigm (Mzama 2003), whose objective is to recenter Africans in African narratives, consciousness, historiography and modes of analysis. It is a theory informed by Harlem Renaissance scholastic discussions about the question of Negroes and Africans in the space of modern society, themed at dismantling racial inferiority in Afro-Caribbeans', Afro-

40

Americans and Africans in Africa. Scholars such as Ivan Van Sertima, Chancellor William, Joseph Ben Joachanan, Molefe Kete Asante, Marimba Ani challenges the Eurocentric modes of life narratives and the way of thinking which distorts the presence of Africans in history of civilization. In the context of Kemetic historiography, Cheikh Anta Diop, he debunks the existing historical narratives about Egypt, in line with Afrocentric analysis to recover the Kemet narratives to real owners of history, black people as the champions of civilization (Clarke 2003). The long gone debate of Africa as a continent without history, Africans as people without soul provides new scholarship in the ghetto of Harlem, breeds new kinds of historians, who dares not to go beyond or criticise the existing Euro-American discourse of analysis as to trace the genealogies of civilization which evidence the African pedigree of world civilizations.

"The Europeans learned in the fifteenth and the sixteenth centuries that you cannot successfully oppress a consciously historical people because a consciously historical people will not let it happen" (Clarke 1998; 78)

This historical distortion and de-centering of Africans in African narratives deny their ownership of historical civilization. Clarke (1998) and Ngugi wa Thiongo (2010) questions the discourse of culture, history and language tools used by imperialist to obliterate Africans in the map of global history of civilization. John Jackson, Alvin Boyd, Godfrrey Higgins, Stanley Lane switched on the light in the dark city of Harlem and begin to speak for the African course. In this regard, Afrocentric theory emerge as social and intellectual consciousness themed on centering Africans in narrative of their own history, stories once distorted for several centuries.

"Afrocentric is therefore a consciousness quality of thought, mode of analysis and an actionable perspective where Africans seek from Agency to assert subject place within the context of African history" (Asante 2007;16)

In this regard, the discourse of remembering the dismembered creates wonders on the objective of African emancipation, which is not political project, but an intellectual issue whose aim is to entrench the template of Afrikology (Nabudere 2013) as the best form of knowledge of Africans. It is not Afrocentrism which is a direct opponent to Eurocentric paradigms (Asante 2007), but an independent thinking asserting African agency in African historicity and the way of life. In the context of ghetto as residential area, created by Europeans, is an alien to African indigenous urban systems since it is founded on the principle of social injustices. Amilcar Cabral, remembered for his critical thoughts on the role of culture in revolution, argued that the Europeans manage to subjugate Africans and stole the land as means of production, but the culture remains unchartered and acted as a source of unity. Though the case might be different in Francophone and Anglophone Africa since cultures are nearly destroyed in Francophone, in its complete nature but language, names and ancestral history still provides the glimpse of cultural values to Africans in rural areas and urban ghettos. Rural migrants also preserved cultures and customs, hence urban-rural interface provided a critical challenge to the existence of western modernity in ghetto cosmology. Ghetto cosmology is a revolutionary act legitimised in the same way Negritude by Leopold Senghor defined as Humanism of the 20th Century; it is embedded on cultural residues of indigenous values. The role of music is too tempting to forget, Afro-jazz music and traditional music re-awaken Africa's greatness which aid an Afrocentric incubation of ghetto cosmology. However, the continuation of Euro-modernity to ghetto cosmology is massive, it is not immune to global capitalist structure (Quinjano 2000, Mignolo 2013), though ghetto cultures such as Zimdancehall music is rooted in Afro-Jamaican reggae, western values provides the designs of defining the society, aesthetics and images. The mixture of cultures as informed by the history of Africa's slang is a method of communication conceived in ghetto streets, shipped from Jamaican ghetto but the usage of foreign colonial languages continued. Ghetto beings mostly communicated with mixed languages which clearly showed the increase in the drifting away from the African languages. There is a serious contestations and debates on the usage of English in ghetto streets, but it is legitimised since today there are a various versions of Englishes though rooted from British Imperial rule but carry little or no British cultural components; it is method of communication to bigger audiences (Mazrui 1995), hence ghetto as place where cultures meet, is not free from the high public consumption of foreign languages but remains in the rails of Africanity. Ngugi wa Thiongo (1981) argued that language is a subset of culture, which shows a strong relationship between language and culture, where the language culture is possibly found there is also a product of people's history. Language as the mirror of culture as it explained by Ngugi wa Thiongo providing an understanding of how Shona or Indigenous languages are relegated to the margins of public communication in ghetto, If one is heard speaking ChiManyika,

He/she labelled 'wasu', but it reflects a mockery way for those who speak fluent indigenous languages, accused of being too rural, not fit for urban culture of which rural Africa is the source of culture funds of the banks of the existence of post-coloniality. This reflection of life in ghetto is real and this confusion is rooted in colonial history of the country and the presence of global structure which reflects coloniality of social space. The experiences of linguistic variations challenge the Afrocentric nature of ghetto cosmology, hence it confirms Mudimbe (1988) hypothesis of the tragedy of Africa as invention. Cresswelsing (1991), the increase in demeaning language limits the total prevalence of 'Ubuntu' in ghetto space, whereby the use if vulgar language strips of the concept of humanness in ghetto youth, hence it makes challenges of ghetto cosmology in searching a post-colonial state so complex. The root of it, though explained as a result of mental slavery purports self-hatred in Cresswelsing work, Paul Gilroy (Gilroy 1993) work provides sufficient argument to comprehend the reason behind ghetto confusion. He introduces the philosophical position of 'double consciousness", premised on the historical legacy of African descent in diaspora and even in contemporary Africa. Africans in search of their Africaness have found themselves in the strange world social constructed by the western world, which means the cultural connection of African and the present social space instead of creating a true Afrocentric being, it creates 'double consciousness'. This philosophical position challenge the Africanity nature of ghetto cosmology, but the theory of Afrocentric accepts the metaphysical existence of other templates of knowledge outside the African tradition, which cannot be ignored due to growing connection of different societies in the world.

Conclusion

The relations between ghetto being and ghetto space, is the cultural development. As a resultant of ghetto conditions, which characterised abject poverty, colonially created and poor service delivery ghetto cosmology emerge as human-liberation project founded on the principle of liberty. In post-colonial state, ghetto culture spread beyond geographical location, conquering rural youth and low density suburb youth as post-nationalistic movement speaking for the rights of the subaltern. Ghetto cosmology blended in modern Afrocentric theoretical propositions to be a fully-fledged emancipatory discourse whose aim is to liberate ghetto youth bodies, mind and soul of the current global capitalistic project.

Chapter Four
Image of Post-Colonial Ghetto Renaissance

Abstract

Africa experiences the dark ages, more than five centuries of intellectual vacuum characterised by non-existence of pure scholastic invention as a result of Arab conquest, Trans-Atlantic slavery and colonialism. The continent was once great, taught philosophy to the Greeks, Aristotle, Socrates and Plato learned in Kemet but the glory of the past destroyed by the people from the North and East. Post-colonial experience creates a glimpse of renaissance, African art, literature, poetry and music based on Afrocentric paradigm rose into prominence. Ghetto renaissance rescue the glory and cognitive ability of African beings stimulates confidence in the relating with other races, objects and space in the world. This paper mandated to explore the phenomenon of ghetto culture in the context of romantic literary movements. In cultural dynamics, the increase in intellectual capabilities of 'ghetto youth' marks the beginning of creating a post-colonial intellectual project ranging from art, literature and poetry. The main thrust of this paper is to unpack the contextual relations of ghetto culture in Zimbabwe and the emancipatory project, emancipating ghetto youth from mental slavery in European literature, education, music and art. Post-structural and critical social theory employed to inform the arguments of this philosophical position, which reveals that, post-colonial ghetto culture is more of a liberationist and deconstructionist projects through artistry expression. The need to finance these activities transforms not only ghetto youth, but the Zimbabwe post-colonial lived space.

Key Words; Renaissance, Art, Poetry, Music and liberation

Introduction

Why liberationist project? Liberating from who? Why liberation in post-colonial Africa? Is Art, poetry and 'muzik' enough to liberate ghetto youth? These questions provides basis of arguments of this paper, since the mandate is to answer the questions in a logical perspective. The Post-colonial Zimbabwe's hope transformed into melodramic nightmares resulted from the deposition of political violence, political crisis and economic decline. In this regard, ghetto as the haven of public space and political discussions, the increase in unemployed graduate youth rise into a revolution, through art, music and poetry. In an attempt to negotiate space, Zimdancehall music emerge and supersede Afro pop-urban groves and poetry slums to engage with public, rising hopes, and questions the status quo and source of earning to survive in 'ghetto condition' continuing in post-colonial state. This paper is divided into five sections aimed at discussing thoroughly the hypothesis of the relationship between ghetto emerging cultures and emancipation, the issue of continuity of ghetto conditions in colonial discontinuities theatre in public sphere, redemption songs, intellectual development and the mantra of ghetto youth. In search of 'uhuru' or post-colonial space, Ghetto renaissance is proved useful in African self-reclamation and redemption.

Continuity in Discontinuities; Metaphysics of Ghetto Conditions

The so-called colonial discontinuities carry the lethal continuity of colonial ghetto conditions, since freedom is still in chains the changes

47

is the government bureaucrats but the situation is still the same. Post-colonial political sociology instead to mirror the great awakening of the continent, mirrors the colonial state in its function; it inherits the colonial governance structures hence ghetto renaissance calling for decolonial space through arts and literature renaissance. From philosophical point of view, Aristotle's logic confirms that human beings are political animals; hence humans and politics are indispensable. Asante (2000) funds knowledge banks on the claims of epistemic ownership of Greek philosophy as stolen from Africa, an argument raised in 1954 by George James as he argued that the idea of 'humans as political' animal is attracted from the laws of Ma'at which is Kemetic philosophy. From Hobbes point of view, the creation of the polity or political unity is based on dismantling state of nature which described as brutish, nutsy and jungle shaped by human nature. State of nature remains a best possible solution to develop morals, laws and strong government to incarcerate human nature and state of nature as political lived space. In this regard, post-colonial Zimbabwe is a model of social contract philosophy, from pre-colonial political blueprints blended with enlightenment thoughts. The hopes of liberation struggle premised on Marxist dialectical philosophy (Amin 2010) to empower the marginalised or subalterns (Spivak 2010) natives, but the situation that turned around remains the same, those who were in the periphery are still locked there, oppressed by the new black elites referred to neo-capitalism by Sachikonye (2003). Fanon (1967), warn Africans about this, calling it Africanisation whereby the middle class led the revolutions and peasants play a dirty work. Those petty African bourgeoisies, brainwashed by European education rises as new forms of elites, puppets in post-colonial society, became corrupt and continued to subjugate the peasants. This is exactly what happened in post-colonial Africa. ZANU PF regime failed to deliver its promises to the masses due to lack of finances, corruption and authoritarianism. This political environment led to the creation of new forms of revolutionary cultures, questioning the existing quo. The struggles for black emancipation continue in post-independence.

"Are we facing birth pangs or death-pangs in the presence of boundaries of Identity? Are we witnessing the real bloody forces of decolonization as the colonial structures within arbitrary boarders of decaying or collapsing? Is the post-Berlin colonial state being washed clean with the blood of victims, villains and martyrs? Are refugees victims of dying order, or are they traumatised witnesses to an epoch-making rebirth? Is this blood from the womb of history giving painful birth to a new order? (Mazrui 1986)

In the construction of post-colonial thoughts, Mazrui (2010) asked a parade of questions based on the reason why there's is decaying order in Africa and the objectives of struggles for freedom failed to bring positive results at the end of colonialism. In this context, Mazrui (1986, 2000) conceptualises the post-colonial sate based on the questions of emancipation, freedom and independence whereby the condition is so nasty since African body politic is dominated by the assembly of dictators, military coups, serious abuse of human rights and neo-colonialism as the last stage of imperialism. A death pangs of the hopes of democracy and independence. This condition affects the political sociology of Africa's south of Sahara nations, in particular Zimbabwe. Shivji (2009) also argued that, Africa is not yet Uhuru, meaning to say the independence as political reality is an unfinished business in Africa evidenced by the presence of colonialist in means of production and political brutalities by the black governments. Arendt (1994) on the same issue also argued that Africa is in a period of emptiness not yet independent and no longer a colonial state. Another testimonial scholarship is from political scientist and first generation of African scholar (Mkandawire 2010) and Mahmood Mandani analyses logically the pre-independence hopes and the post-colonial political realities.

"Two decades later, we found ourselves in a world for which we ever least prepared. Not only was it a world drenched in blood, but battle lines were hardly inspiring. There was little revolutionary about violence around us" (Mandani 1993; 48)

Mahmood Mandani theorise the post-colonial tragedies, as it was least prepared for since at the eve of Independence people declared the discontinuity of suffering and hope for a better future. Political violence against the poor, peasants and ghetto residents orchestrated shed blood in the map of post-colonial Africa which corroborates Fanon (1967) view of the African bourgeois politics whereby nationalists tend to forget the masses and follow Eurocentric reflections of life. In the Zimbabwean context one party state provided unity between ZAPU and ZANU to avoid civil wars and denigrated the idea of democracy since corruption contributed to the political decay. Economic Structural Adjustment Programme (ESAP) and corruption left the country in serious crisis which led to the increase in labour movements organised by Zimbabwe Congress of Trade Union under the leadership of Morgan Richard Tsvangirai

(Machingambi 2007, Sachikonye 1997, Sachikonye and Raftopolous 2001). Labour movements transformed into political confrontations. This led to the creation of Movement for Democratic Change (MDC) to represent the interest of the workers in ghettos and later white farmers, however the ZANU-PF led government responded ruthlessly, allegedly torturing, detaining and killing opposition supporters in the ghetto and beyond (Sachikonye 2006). Propaganda and violence sponsored to confront the political realities of the popular MDC in urban areas. ZANU PF government failed to deliver economically due to sanctions and mismanagement of funds. According to Moyo (2013), Muchemwa (2013) and Chigora (2008), Zimbabwe was sanctioned as a result of land reform programme which was referred to as a gross violation of human rights, property rights in particular but the aim was to empower blacks. Sanctions and corruption teamed up together and left thousands of unemployed graduates wondering in streets. Most of them joined the post-colonial struggles to deconstruct the existing political landscape. The growth in urban society in Zimbabwe created a new form of a nation, nationalism spoke with one voice towards the political ill of the country. However decolonial sociology questions this form of nationalism and renaissance, since it is compatible with western modernity.

Post-colonial Ghetto Renaissance

In understanding a post-colonial ghetto renaissance, there is needed to take a glance to post-slavery Harlem Renaissance in USA. It is much more similar to ghetto renaissance since it is aimed at addressing the slavery and dehumanization experiences through intellectual project. Harlem Renaissance in the United States of America exists as revolutionary movement in de-campaigning racism, slavery and post-slavery brutalities (Clarke 1998 and 1994). It was characterised by the questioning of the available literature of African history written by the white scholars, since African descents referred to people without history were shipped from the dark continent to the Caribbean and America (William 1992, Clarke 1998). The construction of Eurocentric African historiography challenged in Harlem intellectual discussions developed literature, poetry and music. Scholars such as John Jackson, Marcus Garvey, Stokey Carmichael, John Henrick Clarke, Ivan Van Sertima, Josef Ben Joachanan and Cheikh Anta Diop research on African history and recentering Africans in world history of civilization. This led to civil rights movements, art, poetry, hip-hop music, African fashion designs and literature (Cresswelsing 1991). The main issue was to define 'the density of blackness' as the ontological glory.

Redemption Songs; Post-colonial Ghetto Musik

"Won't you help to sing, the songs of freedom, because all I ever have redemptions songs" (Bob Marley)

The visit of Afrocentric music icon Bob Marley in Zimbabwe in 1980 at Independence influenced the rise of urban-ghetto music suppressed by the popular sungura. Bob Marley and Afro-Jamaican music dubbed as 'black making modern music'. This led to the development of urban grove, blending Afro-Jamaican music, Hip Hop, RnB and also Afro-Jazz icons Oliver Mutukudzi and Thomas Mapfumo also played crucial role. In the early 21st century, Innocent Utsiwegota, Dazebell, Mc Villa to mention a few took music crusades to entertain and speak about contemporary topical issues through music. The main themes were love, speaking less to imminent conditions of ghetto youth. This kind of music divided the society whereby the pre-independence generation listened largely to Sungura and Afro-Jazz, whilst urban groves was mainly attracted to the born free in ghetto and beyond. It also divided the society through socio-geographical differences, rural areas listened more to Sungura, traditional Jiti music and Afro-Jazz whilst urbanites listened to urban groves as reflection of modern life stemmed on the mixture of European modernity and Africanity. The collapse of urban groves around 2008 conceived Zimdancehall music packed in the same Afro-Jamaican roots, but more different to hip-hop inclined urban groves. Winky D, Freeman, Platinum Prince, Blot, Enzo I Shall, Soul Jah Love, Killer T to mention few, excite the public, receives more attention from 'ghetto youth'. However the music was accused of being childish, associated with drugs and its lyrical content contains vulgar, despite this criticisms it continues to conquer the public space, since it is used to negotiate space for ghetto youth in post-colonial Zimbabwe. Zimdancehall unites 'ghetto youth' and form strong youth movements in arts and deconstructionist projects. Chill spot Records in Mbare and other studios, accentuate the eminent rise of the music as youth oriented, aimed at emancipating the youth from ghetto conditions. It is a form of music renaissance, since in Harlem Hip-Hop emerged as emancipatory music, which is the same as Zimdancehall.

Philosophical Aesthetics in Negotiating Space; Poetry and Art

Ghetto renaissance replicate Harlem renaissance, whereby the escalation of 'unemployed graduates does not explain the death of the community; it signifies the decay of production but marks the beginning of community's intellectual projects such as poetry slums, art and literature. Chenjerai Hove, Hamilton Modekai Hamutyinei, Musayemura Zimunya, Dambudzo Marechera, Aaron Chiundura Moyo, A. C. Hodza and Charles Mungoshi are known heroes of the pen, but now there is increase in the army of intellectual movement, redefines the discourse of Zimbabwe's Identity, Politics and Beyond from 'ghetto streets'. Poetry slums in ghettos developed revolutionary minds to ghetto youth, House of Hunger Poetry Slum, Nhaka TV, Chaminuka College Arts and Bust Stop TV took a centre stage to discuss Zimbabwean issues in-depth through poetry and plays as to send voice to the government about the marginalisation of the youth. Poetry and theatre is more revolutionary, aimed at making sense of post-colonial Zimbabwe, but it is also welcomed as renaissance movement since in pre-independence the country produced few poets due to the colonial circumstances. In the basis of literature, once known weaver press and college press publish a volume of literature, but the ghetto streets as Harlem of Zimbabwe breeds writers and publishers of fiction, short stories and poetry. Mwanaka Media Publishing has done numerous work to publish literature speaking about youth, for instance Ghetto Symphony; Anthology of Streets writings in Zimbabwe edited by Mandla Mavolwane, *Zimbolicious: An Anthology of Zimbabwe Literature and Arts* edited by Tendai Rinos Mwanaka, *Mad Bob Republic: Blood Line, Bile and A Crying Child Struggle Poems by* Tendai Rinos Mwanaka explains the ghetto conditions, experiences and the political culture in Zimbabwe. Apart from Knowing Tsitsi Dangarembga, Yvonne Vera and Dambudzo

Marechera as authors of ghetto conditions, Mwanaka Media Publishing breeds new army of ghetto narrators to communicate the revolutionary message. Art and Painting demonstrates youthful talents and modern African aesthetics. In this regard, this ghetto renaissance is a wonder in Zimbabwe, breathes life to the public intellectualism and informs the literary developments towards the future.

Conclusion

The discourse of ghetto youth, formulates a nationalistic movement towards the inclusive-plural society, the discourse is not geographically limited to ghetto residents, and it extends beyond to rural areas as a culture. However, its main purpose is a consumed hope in the sense that youth are still marginalised, in most cases denied of their rights. The Ministry of Youth, NGGS and Youth Council are there as institutions, but failed to give a critical help to deliver youth projects, liberate them from autocratic systems and denied them opportunity. They remained hopeless, increases the influx migration of youth from Zimbabwe to Europe, Asia, America and neighbouring countries in search of greener pastures. But the most important issue in imagining post-colonial Zimbabwe is ghetto youth renaissance mapping the contour of music and scholastic development of the country.

Chapter Five
Reimagining the Post-colonial Ghetto Being in Zimbabwe: Soliciting Football

Abstract

The image of post-colonial ghetto, painted by the youth, not only concentrated on dancehall music but as football fanatics. The relationship between ghetto youth and football extended beyond comprehensive image, and rose as a form of new religion, and a cult which unites ghetto youth. This paper, aimed at interrogating the legacy of football in psychological ghetto being, and how it nourishes ghetto consciousness in post-colonial Zimbabwe. Football followers increase in every corner of the ghetto, though the area has little literature but it invites the author to employ a critical analysis to the determinant of the discourse of space, being and soul through entertainment. This new culture is now a popular culture in the society hence it demonstrates that it is a source of unity, optimism and entertaining objective.

Key Words, Football, Post-colonial ghetto

Introduction

Post-colonial Zimbabwe, a synergy of hope to the former colonised society promotes the talents through football. The legacy of football heroes such as George Shaya, Peter Ndhlovu, Moses Chunga just to mention a few are credited in ghetto spaces for the development of these glorious talents and the spread of names, not only in Zimbabwe but around the world. Foreign footballers also dominate football and argument in ghetto, mostly Cristiano Ronaldo-Lionel Messi debate divide the society in two and dominate the ghetto space. Football legends such as Pele crowned King of Football, Diego Maradona known for his golden hand score, Ronaldinho known for his brilliant skills and dribbles and Ronaldo as the brilliant striker accentuates the rise of the soccer revolution in ghetto streets across the world. The question remains, how important is football? And how it invades ghetto space, relating with ghetto being and post-colonial ghetto culture? These questions shapes the arguments of this paper, relating it to the political realities of Zimbabwe and the context of globalisation. There is a new social epiphenomenon which dominates the society, a globalised football connects the world but at the same time aid global coloniality hence this paper is mandated to unpack those metaphysical situations towards a post-humanistic society. This paper is divided into three, (1) explaining soccer in ghetto streets and domestic leagues, (2) unpack the realities of globalised football and (3) interrogate the psychological implication of soccer to ghetto being.

Theatre of Dreams in Ghetto Streets; Ghetto Consciousness

Power of streets Soccer

From post-structural point of view, power ceases not only to be materially oriented but goes beyond on the trajectory of knowledge, interpretations, cultures and social conditions. The relationship between power and social conditions demonstrated in entertainment as a means of creating unity, consciousness and a powerful society for revolution. In this context, football is not just a source of entertainment but a method of creating power, universal power in the pretext of solidarity. The context of street football in ghetto is largely influenced by two glorious world cups, demonstrates the increase in football proficiency around the globe. The one won by France in 1998 and the other won by Brazil in 2002 created a spark plug to affection of football around the world, from Dakar to Soweto. Streets as the strategic areas of ghetto provides a much needed fertile ground for the development of ghetto cosmology and a space for football revolution. In most cases streets used as play grounds with bricks as gates, playing barefooted, shirtless for identification and using plastic man-made balls, others are given names of great players and defines ghetto street football's culture. This aspect of the reflection of ghetto life portrays a critical phenomenon which pave the way for cementing ghetto consciousness, it drills to the ghetto youth through street football, and promotes belongingness. This environment is not just a mere lived space, but promotes ghetto consciousness. Apart from music street football trains the minds of the 'ghetto youth' the sense of belonging and believes in unity as an important discourse in post-colonial state. According to Temples (1953), Wiredu (2002) and Appiah (2010), Ubuntu philosophy is premised on a cosmos perspective of " I am because we are" which means to street football as a source of ghetto consciousness, creates a collective identity and the virtue of being and belonging to a certain community as one of the highest desires of human soul. Street football narrows ghetto culture since it confines it to high density residential and rural areas since low density suburbs is little exposed to this kind of culture. In this regard, it explains the existence of serious social inequalities in post-colonial Zimbabwe. Streets is where ghetto spirits dwells, not evil spirits but connecting souls; bodies of youths to believe in unity as a result of team building activities such as sports. It is believed that Brazil football emanated from the ghettoes of Rio de Jeneiro, Sao Paulo and Brasilia, and most prominent footballers in Zimbabwe are products of street soccer. Ghetto has so many things to offer than drugs, the growing inequality in Zimbabwe continues to marginalise high density suburbs, but a lot of talents are hidden there, ghetto consciousness is a revolutionary act, shapes the thinking of youth as one, experience the same ghetto conditions.

Domestic League; Social Dialogue through Football

Dialogue explains social relations, how one relates to the world with others, objects and space. Street football is the starting point and develops into a professional league. As a unifying factor it now unite cities towards a post-colonial liberation project. Zimbabwe Football Association (ZIFA) is a regulatory body, register teams, promotes the sport and monitor the activities, and as a body it paves the way to the creation of professional leagues ranging from division one up to Castle Premier League. Mostly premier league is more professional and attracts a number of supporters, for instance Dynamos- its home ground in Rufaro Stadium is situated in Mbare, hence as the most successful club in Zimbabwe Football history, its supporters are mainly from Mbare. Highlanders nicknamed Bosso, are situated in Bulawayo and unites ghetto in the city of kings. The most Important discourse in league football is that it is a continuation of street football and promotes nationalistic consciousness stretching from Mbare, Rufaro Stadium as it originated to the supporters to many different ghettos and rural areas. These inter-city, inter-territorial and inter-class connections make a league football different to that of streets, but spread ghetto cosmology across the nation. It is emotional, hilarious, sad but jovial, but sorrowfulness too, to lose or win but the culture remains the same, as aspiration of freedoms and imagining a post-colonial Zimbabwe.

Terra Incognita: Unpacking the Realities of Globalised Football

How football can be globalised? This is an interesting part of the ghetto culture in post-colonial soviet whereby a number of scholars still unexplored this issue but it's too much to ask them. Globalisation has been romanticised by neo-liberal scholars as the last stage of human development to fulfil Hegel Philosophical prophecy, attesting that human beings develop from primitive to a more civilised, which is witnessed by the increase in peace consciousness as post-world wars reasoning. Fukuyama (1992) put it in that way, the collapse of USSR as a threat to world peace through its communistic ideas marked the triumph of liberalism which connects the whole together and eliminates wars. He calls it end of history, but it invites numerous criticism since the universal empire portrayed by Fukuyama disadvantaged other cultures, facilitated the clashes of civilisation (Huntington 1996) which led to wars and strengthened the project of global coloniality. For Fukuyama (1992) (Gilpin 2010), the post-historic society formed on top of the corpses of state security, fascism, protectionism and communism to show the triumph of western modernity in the name of liberalism. Ghetto as colonial construct, affected by the whirlwind, continues to strip African culture naked. Globalisation is the interconnectedness of the global society through culture, technology and trade. This interconnectedness work in favour of 'imperial being' (Dusell 1980),

60

since how can it be global if it is situated from Euro-American modernity (Ndhlovu-Gatsheni 2013, Quinjano 2000, Mignolo 2013). In this regard, it is agreed the globalisation is a new form of imperialism continuing to universalise western modes of thinking, western ideas as truth and hierarchize the global society. How it relates to football? What is it significant to contemporary ghetto culture? These questions construct a logical framework of comprehending the philosophical convictions of globalised football. Contemporary football, home or domestic league attracts less people than it used to be in early independence period, there are few supporters of Highlanders in Zimbabwe than that of Manchester United. Domestic league treated with contempt, as waste of time, due to issues of corruption and lack of professional footballers, less competitive to European Football. English Premier League, Spanish LaLiga, Italian Seria A, Germany Bundesliga and French League 1 largely followed by ghetto youth, to the extent of wearing jerseys of teams they claim they support. Manchester United, Manchester City, Liverpool, Barcelona and Real Madrid have fans all over the street corner. These clubs are more attractive because of world class players playing professional football than domestic leagues; however this new ghetto culture needs to be scrutinised carefully in the reflection of African self in ghetto being. In some instances it resulted from power of western world to control meanings, information, and media and universalise their society to the other. It is true that there is no supporters of Dynamos in England who are British citizens, but there are supports of Manchester United in Mbare that are Zimbabwean citizens, it explains the clashes of cultures, civilizations and the inferior societies always bow to global civilizational powers. This condition termed Wretched of the Earth in Fanon (1967) works, and ghettoized Africans put faith much in European cultural commodity as always superior to that of Africa. In weekends, bars in ghettos are always packed, youth watch games there. Of course it is colonially rooted or exposes coloniality of being, though some cultures still blended with urban-rural interface to preserve African glory, but the issue of football has a volume of story to tell; embedded on the economic condition of the country. The environment deterministic model is applied to verify the linkages between economic environment and the increase in affection of European football. Unemployed graduates and other youth have nothing to do, fail to trust the government since it has been internalising corruption in football body. Watching European soccer helps ghetto youth to restore hope, re-energize souls from the absurd environment which deny those rights and privileges. Afrocentrism not Afrocentric disfavours the support of the globalised football as an imperialistic agenda, but Afrocentric does not oppose globalised football; it is good to watch football and at the same time support the domestic football in search of post-colonial 'ghetto being'. Entertainment space unspare the development of post-colonial ghetto being, as the central point of imagining post-independence ghetto society.

Psychological Implication of Soccer to 'Ghetto Being'

The philosophical convictions of ghetto space, in the traits of football culture unspare the psychological or noetic dimension of human beings. The psychological situation of ghetto being is aptly captured in ongoing social conditions in Africa, partly in Zimbabwe whereby economic crisis strains the 'psychological being' searching for existence through attaining all required aspects to survive.

Football as on the list of survival strategy play a major role to existentiality of being in the world space, being a football supporter draw soul of relevance in society. It also claims the discourse of belongingness, which is one of the primary requirements to define existence of human, as being in society. Ubuntu cultural cosmology (Temples 1954, Wiredu 2002, Broodryk 2002), the lived space determined by a cultural unit of different individuals in constituting a society were one's identity is derived from a group, it can be said that, "He/she is Shona, because of cultural belonging to the Shona people". The implication of soccer to ghetto social psychology is based on the development of communitarian modes of being; being a Liverpool Fc Supporter it has no individual conviction, but belongs to a group of Liverpool Football Club supporters around the world. The psychological effects of soccer to ghetto being are a critical area, which relates soul with the lived experience solicited by the culture of football. In other case, it also opens the avenues of the will to live, will to survive to defeat the existentiality of the meaningless of life resultant from the economic environment effects of the country. Why the ghetto being choose to follow European football? This question is so important in constructing being, epistemological, in short its because of the search for existence, relevance and belongingness. On the basis of communication, the relationship of the body, space, soul and time of oneself reflects on how effective are modes of equality because soccer is usually watched in bars, taverns-even people have their own televisions at home. It's a culture whereby one leaves his television and the comfort at home, even when he is not an alcoholic, he chooses to watch soccer in noisy packed bar. This kind of situation express uniformity and equivalence in community psychology, and unites different souls as one, chanting one slogan. It is so amazing why such condition become conducive to watch soccer, in ad-hoc researches or social observation, the majority of responses favour watching football in bar or club because of its entertaining space than at home. The psychological implication of the crowded area demonstrates the dialogue of oneself with the community. This is how the reflection of ghetto experience triumphs in post-independence society.

Conclusion

The dynamics of society create a new form of culture, the discourse of football is difficult to ignore, and it is now a part of culture and social norm. It stretches from nucleus level, expands to league and globalised football, but all in all the street football is more fascinating, more realistic since is shapes the social cosmology of the ghetto. It is a revolutionary culture aimed at search 'Zimbabwe' in post-colonial society. However, the Afrocentric nature of ghetto culture on the unit of football is questioned, domestic football is treated as inferior than the so called globalised football, hence what went wrong with domestic league? Where is Zimbabwe in post-colonial society? These questions still explore the gap needed to be filled to sustain Zimbabwe ghettos as revolutionary phenomenon.

Chapter Six
The Soul of Ghetto Space in Mbare

Abstract

Mbare is the birth place of ghetto, ghetto being and cosmology. It is imperative to rethink the discourse of ghetto being through a logical analysis of the birth place of Zimbabwe ghettos. The urban settlement, a historical symbol of colonialism, it is an archive, a repository of the history of colonial administration. It symbolises the death place of African cultures, identity and the triumph of Euro-capitalist6 modernity culture which not produce a conscious 'being' but an 'other' whose ontological existence is subjected to the named alien culture fed by the colonial system of governance. Whose ghetto? Why Mbare? Provides a benchmark of arguments in scrutinise or hermeneutic analysis of 'ghetto space' for existential phenomenon of ghetto being. Mbare endowed with haunting memories on how Africa cease exist, the reflection of multicultural society through immigrants from Malawi during Rhodesia and Nyasaland. The town also enter the post-independence in absentia of post-coloniality due to sprouted Anglo-Saxony modes of thinking which distorts the activities. The question of politics, and service delivery, entrepreneurship and future of the ghetto heritage symbol enables the opening of arguments and discussions of this paper. Meta-analysis of the space, goes beyond a glory understanding of ghetto being, but traces a dialogue relational of the living conditions and human beings as the ingredients of social values

Key Words, Mbare, Ghetto Being, Soul

Introduction

After successive colonial process, the pioneer Colum hoist the flag in Salisbury, now Harare and construct a new urban residential area, which is today is the oldest ghetto, a historic city archived with the memories of how Zimbabwe was forcefully taken from Ndebele people and Shona people. Mbare as the oldest ghetto is a historic town symbolises the beginning of effective colonial administration by the British. Mbare become the haven of ghetto activities, whereby serious migration from rural areas and beyond boarders populates the city in search of selling labour to the nearby industry in exchange of the so called salary, which was also enough to sustain livelihood hence this kind of work was more exploitative and degrades the labour rights of the native. In analysing ghetto being, space and culture Mbare is the starting point, house colonial and post-colonial experiences in reality terms. A labour city, populated with different ethnic groups, especially from Malawi who continue their gule wamkulu cultures and also Islamic cultures. This is not end there, the rural migrant also continue in cultural expression of the Shona people, such as Mbira playing and various customs. Though the creation of urban settlement was at the same time de-tribalisation, alienation to indigenous cultures and dislocation from the roots it provides space for expressing the little cultural existence in a multicultural tolerance. This historical experience and situation, breeds a new cultural legacy based on mixed bag of cultures, languages at the same time influenced by European cultural traditions. However, racism injected whereby Mbare ghetto was restrictedly for blacks only, and there some restrictive areas in town and low density suburbs whereby blacks were not allowed, the communication discourses were not equally, bass-boy relations defines the racial systems continue to purge the confidence of Africans, make them objects and inferior. Mbare is a historic city, a soul of ghetto. This paper aimed to explore the relevance of Mbare in the creation of ghetto being and culture, informed by the history and contemporary experiences. It also aimed at explaining experiences of Malawi migrants, their contact with Shona-Ndebele cultures which resulted into formation of identities some of them based on reality and other just an imagination, Labels, stereotypes and images created which shapes ghetto being based on the migrant experiences. Mbare is the largest market place in Zimbabwe, and this paper explores the challenges, context and prospects of the Mabare economic activities as the survival strategies of the ghetto youth. In post-colonial projections, the inadequate service delivery and corruption become a human rights concern which is not to be ignored in this essay. Above all, the main theme of this essay also premised on searching the post-colonial state, whereby Zimbabwe is not yet post-colonial, so Mbare as the soul of the ghetto the author provides a decolonial alternatives for establishing a genuine post-colonial perspective. In this regard, space, realities and lived experiences are the sources of establishing the existentiality discourse of ghetto being, hence Mbare ghetto selected to broaden the scope through named themes to be discussed.

Confirming From History: Methodological and Historiographical Problems of the History of Mbare

The present literature of the history of Zimbabwe, put a little focus on the historical legacy of Mbare, though historians include it as the starting point of labour and capital in colonial Zimbabwe, whereby

Dean Botts present it in "Labour in Colonial Zimbabwe" but there is injustice in the historical records of the city. In this sect6ion, the author is not a historian but a trained social scientist which means theories of Afrocentric Social science applies to construct a histrorico-analytico discourse of the history of Mbare. Before taking a journey of the historical analysis of the creation of Mbare as the first urban settlement, the history of colonialism is important to inform the arguments. Lord Macaulay is a historic figure in understanding the methodologies of colonialism, experiences and the anti-colonial struggles in Africa (Raftopolous 1994, Vambe 1980).

> "I have travelled across the length and breadth of India and Africa not seen person who is a beggar, who is a thief such wealth I have seen in this country, such high moral values, people of such calibre, that I do not think we would ever conquer this country, unless we break the very backbone of this nation, which is her spiritual and cultural heritage and therefore, I propose that we replace her old and ancient education system and English is good and greater than their own, they will lose their self-esteem, their native cultures and they will become what we want them, a truly dominated" (Lord Macaulay's Address to the British Parliament on 2 February 1835)

This famous speech is largely analysed by scholars across the globe, and rated as the best speech accentuate colonialism through is social condition presentations, problems associated with colonial motives to the people of the south and the methods of conquest. The problematic discourse of this speech is that, it came at the same time where Valladolid Judgement deny humanity of Africans in favour of La Casas, Hegelian historisophical analysis of the western beings, orients and Africans which creates a hierarchy whereby a European being viewed as scientific, an orient and progressive being and African as the person with sense but intelligence in absentia. It was also the same era, whereby Immanuel Kant introduces a racial analysis in anthropology as the study of primitive society which is Africa (Bessie 2010), and also that was Trevor Roper once describe Africa as people without historical conscience which conceive the nomenclature of Africa a "Dark Continent". All these point of view where racist, but Lord Macaulay end introduce a pragmatic concept of truth who there are. He praises Africa and Orients cultural values, whereby described as no burgers which define a highest civilised nation and cultural conscious people. It is difficult to conquer cultural conscious people, as presented by Clarke (1998), since culture is the symbol of unity, nationalism in doing so culture were demonised (Lezra 2010) following Macaulay methodical propositions. This historical speech used by different government in conquest whereby French conquest was based on total cultural demonization through the process of assimilation, Fanon (1963) and Maldonado-Toress (2017) also provides a critical account of assimilation based on (1) linguistic nationalism, (2) cultural alienation and (3) racial superiority policies which erases self-esteem the natives. The British did not totally exterminate culture but dehumanise (Mazrui 1986). In this regard, blacks reduced as objects. In the colonial history of Zimbabwe, Dutch failed to establish control since they did not realise the cultural strength of the people, but British succeed after the signing of Rudd Concession. Lobengula signature inaugurates the new era, new stories unfolds in the land between Limpopo and

Zambezi, the creation of colonial administration after the unsuccessful anti-colonial resistance led by Mbuya Nehanda and Kaguvi described as first Chimurenga 1896-99. The culture glorified by Lord Macaulay demonised, beggars increased and violence begun. In 1907, the area under Chief Harava which later corrupted to Havarari (Harare), the first ghetto created, ghetto of beggars, came to beg for a piece of silver to survive which was alien to African cultures, in thousands of years of the history of the continent. Mbare constructed, whereby hostels and flats constructed to cater for male labourers who migrates from rural to urban in search of employment. As the early ghetto, it provides adequate stories of colonial brutalities and evils, whereby those close packed hostels in Magabha and Matapi housed thousands of black male labourers. Sean Botts explained it adequately that Mbare was formed for labour reservoir, Fanon (1963) and Maldonado-Toress (2018) discourses of the zones of human being and zones of non-beings projected. That is to say, Mbare experiences and its metaphysical existence reflects the zones of non-beings in colonial times, natives demonised, reduced to objects, subjected to labour abuses just to earn living and take care of the family in rural areas. The society was demarcated, whereby areas such as Mount Pleasant were for whites only. This social inequality reflects the Imperial-capitalistic tradition act in the advantage of the colonisers. In the studies of the colonial establishment of urban residents and the experiences of the blacks presented well by Manganyi (1974) in the book, "Being Black in the World". He construct the phenomenology experiences of the black workers in apartheid South Africa, whereby dehumanisation was on its highest level since black workers denied rights to join trade unions as security measures to avoid black protests, blacks dehumanised and forced to be crowded in Soweto ghetto as labour reservoirs. This situation, as presented as ghetto situations which distorts the image of the blacks, devour black self-esteem however it creates a revolutionary consciousness. In this regard, the situation in Mbare ghetto was also the same, as presented by Manganyi (1974) and these experiences contributed to the creation of black sociological schema embedded on the social realities of absurd and revolution as the alternatives to escape. Mandani (2010) in Citizen and the Subject also present the concept of detribalisation, bifurcated societies which problematized the revolutionary consciousness. Ghetto residents in Mbare were de-tribalised from their ethnic society, dislocated from their roots and alienated from their cultures, stripped their humanity and lost self to be characterised as the other. Though the glimpses of cultures prevails, the strong colonial force bequeath it, creates non-thinking ghetto beings, who fear "bass" and fear imposed to them as to crush demonstrations. The news of Soweto and Sharpeville massacre impose more fear as social control to the urban dwellers, much appreciation to rural people who were acquainted to cultures and fought the liberation struggle, not to liberate the country only but to liberate black in urban areas as colonial asylums. In this regard, the history of Mbare as the ghetto soul, the oldest ghetto is important in understanding the relationship between experiences and existentiality, since Mbare ghetto space breeds fear, a detribalised being and non-thinking object brainwashed as a result of the working conditions reflects the dichotomy of bass-boy relations, construct white racial superiority. The city is a symbol of colonial historical legacy, even though some of them were stripped their self-esteem but revolutionary consciousness prevails especially from the Marxist readers influences industrial action and the likes of Thomas

Mapfumo express colonial displeasure through music performed in Shabins to instil a revolutionary consciousness.

Immigrants Social Relations: Reflections of Social Politics to Malawi Immigrants in Mbare

There is few literature largely focuses on the reflection of the Malawi Immigrants in Rhodesia and post-independence Zimbabwe. Of course many scholars have analysed it but in passing focusing on their historical construction objectives. Historians such Bhebhe (1988), Cobbings (1990), Samkange (1980) and Ranger (1985) research extensively on the history of Zimbabwe, using different historical methodologies to provide scientific arguments of the stories of Zimbabwe, though in historiography the existence of objective history is denied. Ranger (1985) and other notable Zimbabwean historians accentuates the existence of nationalistic historiography, a history of nationalism and liberation struggle which later criticised by Ranger (2004) as patriotic history, used as weapon through media, newspapers and school history syllabus for ZANU PF to survive, but that kind of history though politically subjective there is little theoretical analysis of the reflections of the Malawi immigrants in Zimbabwe. And also it reflects the problematic discourse of the construction of immigrant's history, since there is not only Malawi but also people from Mozambique, Zambia and other neighbouring countries. Daimon (2018 and 2007) is the leading scholars in the studies of the Malawi migrants, his researches ranging from the starting point of migration, settlements, cultural expression and post-colonial society. His researches based on story accounts, experiences of the Malawi immigrants and general observations. The federation of Rhodesia and Nyasaland marks the new era of Zimbabwe's social history, since like rural-urban migrant came to urban areas in search for employment as source of income, Malawi, mainly Chewa group emigrates from Nyasaland to Rhodesia and establish permanent settlement. Most of them begin to own houses in Mbare, establish permanent settlements. But it led to serious social conflicts emanated from the construction of stereotypes and labels (Daimon 2008 and Mashiri 2010). There were labelled "MaBhurandaya" that is to say people from Blantyre capital of Nyasaland, "ManYasarandi" meaning people from Nyasaland and other social labels. In the systematic philosophy of social relations, the metaphysical location and being are closely related to create an identity concept or onomastic to refer to certain people, that the same with Malawi immigrants, those labels there were given in Mbare ghetto residential space was related to the metaphysical location of their original homelands. They continue to express the matrilineal cultures, Gule wamkulu or Nyau Dance (Daimon 2007) as expression of their cultures hence Mbare become the hub of multicultural. As black people, they experience colonial brutalities but double barrelled since even the native Zimbabweans also segregate them but most of them participate in war of liberation struggle and post-colonial national building. The inter-marriages and perpetuities of colonial brutalities unite these two ethnic groups in a shared mutual knowledge of colonial suffering. Malawi immigrants also introduces Islam in Mbare as dominant religions, since they were exposed to Islam as religious redemption of the soul, the majority of the Malawi descendants are Muslims, hence Mbare ghetto space was the hub of multicultural expressions. In post-colonial ghetto, Malawi descendants are still treated as aliens, so who is a Zimbabwe? This problematize the context of nationalism with the prism of Pan Africanism (Ndhlovu-Gatsheni 2009), since those immigrants fought for Zimbabwe, suffer at the hands of colonialist and join anti-colonial struggles but because history tell that there are from Nyasaland used as point to deny them full citizenship, which means there are relegated in political position whilst there constitute a big minority group in Zimbabwe. It the presentation of injustices, the question of who is Zimbabwe? Becoming Zimbabwe (Mlambo and Raftopolous 2009) still dominates, provides a debates on various standpoint however in this paper it is argued that, there are Zimbabweans, not diaspora or immigrants but citizens of the country since some of them were born here, others build up to four generations.

Entrepreneurship, Market and Trajectory of Zimbabwe Economy

The birth of Zimbabwe was from the painful struggle, washed by the bloods of the saints and the freedom fighters who losts their lives in battle grounds. The country inherit functional economic system, though it was capitalistic centred. The adoption of ESAP and 2002 famine cripple the economy, and ghetto life become hard again which transpires into series of Industrial actions organised by Zimbabwe Congress of Trade Union (Machingambi 2007, Sachikonye 2003 and Makumbe 2009). Economic Structural Adjustment Programme (ESAP) policy for designed by World Bank and International Monetary Fund to fund developing countries development projects, but states conditioned to follow certain terms such as devaluation of currency, deregulation (privatisation of economy) and democratisation. Escobar (2002) in post-development theory established to de-centre the interpretation of development from the West as global metropole criticise ESAP as purely capitalistic-exploitative project since those terms are unfavourable to the emerging economies, resulted to harm than good and dependency. This is true, whereby Rodney (1974) Afro-west relation analysis prescribed in the notion of exploitation, which led to development of underdevelopment. This SAPS costs not only Zimbabwe economy, but the whole of Sub-Saharan and left country in serious economic hardships. Civil war in DRC drains much of the resources of the country which creates political vulnerability of the incumbent regime and later led to the rise of Movement for Democratic Change as political opponent (Makumbe 2009). Beginning the post-millennium era, Zimbabwe was sanctioned by USA and European Union over controversial land reforms alleged for violating property rights (Muchemwa 2013, Mutizira 2008, and Ndhlovu-Gatsheni 2009) and also corruptions also led to serious economic decline in Zimbabwe. As a result, ghetto space realities become so absurd, whereby number of people migrates to other countries such as South Africa, Botswana, Namibia and United Kingdom in search of greener pastures, unemployment and living standards skyrocketed. Mbare as the market place remains the hub of activities and provides survival strategies to survive in the harsh economic environment. Small businesses, selling farm products and flea markets rescue people of the economic morass bedevil the country.

Public Service and Corruption: A Human Rights Concern?

The Mbare post-menopausal continue to grow old, City of Harare failed to provide genuine service delivery as a result of the contemporary economic crisis. Politicisation of city council governance structures manifest in form of the councillor offices and major as political positions, elected by the public and representing different political groups. This situation is a bomb itself, explode in every developmental policy to be launched by the council, taking into consideration the composition of Harare City Council councillors majority of them are MDC politicians and the Minister of Local Governance is a ZANU cadre hence the clashes of interest compromise genuine service delivery, everything becomes political. Thornhill (2012) argued that, there is nothing role with politics-public administration dichotomy, but the problem manifests when public institutions are politicised, whereby it reduced to serve political interest rather than public interest. In this regard, the city of Harare is largely pollicised, reduced to serve political interest rather than public interest which also left it vulnerable to corruption. The politicisation of public administration erase professionalism through institutionalising corruption, mismagemnet of funds since nepotism and politics of patronage characterise the appointment procedures (Chikerema 2013). This condition, led to serious poor service delivery evidenced by the burst of sewage in streets, poor sanitation, Mbare sometimes goes for weeks without water and various activities which expose the ghetto to diseases. It is noted that, every cholera outbreak claim lives in Mbare at a higher rate, not because people are not hygienic but the conditions expose them to deadly diseases which goes back to poor service delivery by the city of Harare. As post-menopausal city, her immune system is weak hence there is need a serious sanitation care to maintain her beauty and life span. It is a human rights concern, since Operation Murambatsvina once declared a clean-up activities demolish illegal settlement and restore cities beauty, but political commentators argued that it was a way to scare away MDC supporters in urban settlement (Makumbe 2009, Vambe 2015), United Nations declare it an abuse of human rights, abuse of right to shelter. The city council failed to provide shelter to the people. It also denies right to life since it expose people health hazards.

Mapping the Decolonial Context of Mbare

Do Africans exist? Do Zimbabweans exist? These questions threaten the existentiality of ghetto being in Mbare, since there are various considerations to define the existence of a people, a cultural group and society. Ngugi wa Thiongo (1983) states that, culture is a symbol of existence, so if culture is erased from the people there existence as people is also threatened. It is true that, Africans exist before colonialism due to cultural existence, but at the colonial onset the existence of them (Africans) as cultural conscious group was threatened even removed, since they lost self and become the other, objects work on imposed cultures. In this regard, the existence of African being is questioned, though the contemporary culture is informed by triple heritage which pre-colonial, colonial and post-colonial (Mazrui 1986 and Nkrumah 1967) influence by Africa's tradition, Arab-Islam and colonialism. This historical construction of African people still justify their existence but in an incomplete version. The self-hate anti-Africanism portrays a sad image to the Africans as cultural people, since Hollywood cultures erode the struggling existing African cultures; the last values preserved are destroyed. However, on discourse of Zimbabwe identity it is defined by the existence of Chimurenga cultures and the establishment of revolutionary cultures which was once fighting colonialism and focuses on political repression. Mbare as the soul of ghetto space is not immune to decolonial philosophy, number of residents are cultureless which enable one to replay history on how the native Africans urban areas were detribalised, lost cultural identities and emulates Anglo-Saxony Cultures.

"My point is that the only authentic identity for the Africans is tribe. I am Nigerian because a Whiteman created Nigeria and gave me identity. I am black because Whiteman constructed black to be as different as possible from his white. But I was Igbo before the white man come" (Ngozie Adichie 2006)

As presented by Chimamanda Ngozie Adichie, this is how Africans lost the meaning of their belongingness, tribes and ethnic society since their identities are colonially constructed. This is the same with Zimbabwe; its boarders are colonially created, but the rich cultural system in the nomenclature Zimbabwe show the existence of the glimpse of cultural glory to aid revolution in post-imperial society. Mbare is also populated by Malawi immigrants, some of them losts their cultures totally, of course cultures are dynamics but the situation of immigrants cannot describe the changes of cultures due to cultural erosion sourced from colonialism, coloniality and Pax-Americana projects. Pax-American simply means the universalisation of American values. In this regard, the identity of being Zimbabwean to the immigrants and natives must be meaningful, decolonised to create a revolutionary consciousness based on cosmos values of being human in decolonial praxis. Mbare public space need to be decolonised opened up for cultural expressions and unlocks the secrets knowledge of African medicines. The ghetto is a hub of entertainment activities such as Zimdancehall music at Chllspot studio, poetry slums, theatre at Mai Musodzi Hall and other places as well as home of prestigious Dynamos Football Club at Rufaro Stadium, hence it is prudent to decolonise Mbare public space through creating Afrocentric consciousness in studio, art performing halls and entertainment spaces to promote the brand being African. Ghetto cosmology is not narrowed to a revolutionary culture challenge the existing governance structures but confronting the unjust cognitive world seeded in colonial times and maintained by coloniality. The city is a symbolises Zimbabwe history, hence must take part in decolonise ghetto being

Conclusion

Mbare is the soul of ghetto, an oldest ghetto, a birth place of ghetto being and culture which is beyond racial lines, cultural differences and gender differences. Mbare is the birth place of the concept and a possible beigest player in ghetto renaissance as intellectual, revolutionary and political project to challenge the existing leadership, social livelihoods and coloniality of being. Mbare analysed as house of many, since Malawi culture never totally cease to exist, Nyawo dance provides a unique African rhythm of the body and its lyrical context as pure African to liberate from political regression and Eurocentric modes of life. The city is also affected by poor service delivery as a result of incompetent bureaucrats.

Chapter Seven
Pentecostal Myth; the Soul of Ghetto Being

Abstract

In constructing what is called ghetto being, the experiences are not forgotten since there are critical sources to the existence of being, this paper explores ghetto space through Pentecostal experience as somehow a soul to ghetto being, which is remembered as once referred to people without soul. Post-colonial culture is not necessarily informed by politics though Aristolean logic refers to human beings as political animals but it is transcended to religious experience as unit in political decisions, whereby the ever-changing religious reformation hit Christianity, this time not in Christian-Protestant wars, but a more eloquent Pentecostal revivals. Though Pentecostalism develops in the early 20th century, it fully establishes itself in 21st century. In Zimbabwe, ghetto was the haven of social activities, remains a fertile ground for Pentecostal development. The main thrust of this paper is to examine the relationship between ghetto soul and Pentecostal myth, going beyond the scope of religion, but engaging in deliverance from poverty; striking in the country, mass prayers, mass mobilisation and spiritual revival as exorcist methods. Ghetto as Europeans constructs; was this methodology to emancipate Africans? Pentecostals managed to mobilise the people, but failed to redeem them, hence a question remains on its emancipatory discourse, in reclamation of 'being' contrary to the existing lesser being reference.

Key words; Pentecostal, myth

Introduction

Is Pentecostal culture a redemptive strategy? Is it a new religious culture aimed at replacing European protestant? What is the relationship between Pentecostal and ghetto being? It is popularly known that Zimdancehall is the fabric of post-independence ghetto culture and universalises it beyond ghetto boundaries. Religion cannot be omitted in the prism of emancipation of ghetto being, as lesser being in global sociology, as the main objective of ghetto, but historically it is proven that religion is used as redemptive strategy even against political oppression. The role of African Traditional Religion is not forgotten as corroborative aspect to the hypothesis of religious role in human liberation. The determinant strategy of religion packed beneath ethical development, whereby Hobbesian theory of state of nature, ungoverned society, develops religions as source of ethics to liberate humans from their selfish, aggressive and greedy behaviours. Christianity, Buddhism, Hinduism, Taoism, Islam and ATR formulated on the basis of providing answers to super natural questions of life, mainly the issue of freedom, questions of death, spiritual relations and existence of God (Mbiti 1999). Pentecostal Christian systems are also aimed at demonstrating power of the existence of God, the relations of being and Holy Spirit and miraculous activities. As widely popular in ghetto, it mobilises the mass to even march better than political parties, and attempt to answer the unanswered questions in ghetto streets. Ghetto condition evidenced in the existence of poverty, so people seek redemptions from poverty believing that it came from the misfortunes and ancestral curses. The main theme of this paper is to interrogate the determinants of ghetto space and Pentecostalism over the discourse of reclaiming humanity of the natives in urban areas. The paper seeks to explain Pentecostal historiography, mass mobilisation and questions on its spiritual and physical emancipation in relation to ghetto being, space and cosmology.

Pentecostal Historiography

Pentecostal historiography is the much contested discourse with few materials on how broadly to understand it, however much literature from Togarasei (2005 and 2010), Gifford (1998) and Maxwell (2006) manage to present the historical development of Pentecostal faith in Zimbabwe, but to trace it more comprehensive, the history of Christianity in Zimbabwe is not needed to be narrated either but to be analysed and confirmed from the writings of Zvobgo (1995). To trace the evolution of Pentecostalism n Zimbabwe there is need to construct the Pentecostal historiography from religious reformation around the 16th century, providing a meaningful and a comprehensive story. Christianity originated in Middle East, Europe spread it to far lands. In this regard Euro-Christianity relationship is more important in this discourse, as informing paradigm facilitates a central point of analysis to the universalisation of European being across all continents (Dussell 1979, Mignolo 2000). Christianity gospel creates avenues or easy passage for European Imperialism, whereby the so called Priest is employed by their governments to demonize cultures of other societies who have their own unique belief systems (Lezra 2010), and replace them with Christianity, preaching Jesus as the Saviour of humankind. The gospel was so convincing, persuasive and even established through force. For instance, in Zimbabwe in colonial period, people were forcefully converted to Christianity, some at the gunpoint. Religious reformation did not necessarily end at 1648 Treaty of Westphalia (Buzan 2010), but it even continued to pillage Africans religious infrastructure since Portuguese and Spanish Catholics managed to establish colonies in America and Africa to deter the spread of Protestantism from Dutch; French and British protestants established colonies in India, Africa and Asia. The interpretation of the Bible led to conflicts, whereby Vatican's blasphemous teachings and corruption distorted the spiritual standpoint of the religion; digressing from original Pauline teachings about Jesus Gospel. Protestants suffered persecution because their teachings were direct aggression to the superiority of Catholic tradition in religion and politics. Scotland, Spain and France once fought Islam in crusades, finally defeated them four hundred years later in 15th century at the fall of Grenada, also suffered a thirty years war to maintain its religious relics against the protestant factions. The Treaty of Westphalia 1648 settled disputes to create sovereignty nations (Bull 1989, Hurst 2014). With the help of Berlin Conference 1884-85 and the popular issue of referring to Africans as 'people without soul' from Hegel philosophical tradition, Catholics and Protestants gained momentum as the facilitators of colonialism (Wynter 2010). Mission centres were opened by both groups. The arrival of Christianity in Zimbabwe marked the beginning of the end, the beginning of religious reformation and massive disappearance of African spirituality, demonized and referred to as religions belonging to the dark world. In this regard the hard colonial times and racism was provided by eloquent pastors to challenge the existing social order, for instance in the United States of America, Martin Luther King Junior challenged racism and employed Ghandian non-violence ethics on civil rights movements based on demonstrations and boycott. In Zimbabwe, Reverend Ndabanhingi Sithole also joined the pilgrimage for religious reformation to define the fate of Africans, being in the world. Soweto ghetto was also blessed with Steve Biko's Black consciousness paraded in establishing a mutual consciousness of being black not as just skin colour but a condition of suffering worsened by apartheid, also drilled in black minds as natural settings of racial classification, also developed a wing of Black Theology facilitated by the Anglican Priest, Desmond Tutu. Black consciousness, an intellectual movement, diagnosed the society in the same view point with Frantz Fanon view of colonization of information, behaviour and mind which distorted black's relations with objects, space and time. Of course trained black priests, bishops and reverends spend time in revising the existence of European superiority over Africoids, but actively involved in the politics of liberation and challenging the European systematic theology. The struggle within the protestant and Catholics religion over the question of natives extended to new form of religious values, fighting imperialism through religion, joining ATR and Christianity as a method of pleasing God. The metaphysics of religious existentialism in colonial times led to the formation of quasi-Pentecostal religion such as Johane Masowe, Johane Marange, Apostolic Church and Zion. These churches, though factions increase spontaneously at a faster rate, were attended by native Africans in ghetto as indigenous churches formulated for the cause of liberation. They mobilised the mass, question the existing status quo, prophecy and redefine the context of God in humanity (Mbiti 1963). But as far as history is concerned, Pentecostal historiography present a problem solved by Togarasei (2006) arguing that, Johane Masowe and Johane Marange sects, influenced by the existence of Pentecostalism though took a different theological aspect. In this regard, this religious reformation whereby Indigenous churches attracted peasants not middle class after redemptive strategy, yet Pentecostal came into being and attracted the whites and middle class who believed in social justice. Around 1930s, Apostolic Faith Mission (AFM), a mother of all Pentecostal churches and African Assembly of God (ZAOGA) the 'young zealot' opened, influenced by the deepening crisis of the religious reformation and drew its legitimacy from the Day at Pentecost and Azusa Street Revival. These churches introduced new doctrines, contrary to the traditional Christian Catholic ethics but strictly remained the lenses of the teaching of Jesus Christ. Through anti-colonial Pentecostal churches strictly maintained to the teaching of Jesus Christ. Mass prayers, exorcism, speaking in tongues and prophecy were main features of this religion, though not too political like Catholics and Indigenous Churches, but they managed to attract large audiences, of all classes of the society, calling for redemption, speaking the word of God as it is written mainly in New Testament. In this regard, this historical analysis clearly shows the role of religion in human emancipation, as its confirmed from Christian historiography, to the development of new forms of faith, sharing the same Bible but with different approaches to the external world. As philosophical praxis, whose aim is to influence the society adhere to social values as prescribed in the Bible. Ghetto culture is largely linked to Pentecostalism since the middle class and peasants defined the composition of the religious movement.

Pentecostalism: A Mass Mobilisation Strategy?

Is Pentecostalism a mass mobilisation strategy in ghetto space and culture? In search of the relationship between the Pentecostal experience, ghetto lived-space and ghetto being the above question is not immune to this hypothetical discourse. Revisiting the history of religious reformation in Zimbabwe, Indigenous Churches from onset attracted large followers and became a source of political discussion, merging political strategy with prayers, mostly confirming to prophecy, though rejected to be non-scientific. But the force of Pentecostalism was irresistible whereby its call for universal justice, redemption and back to the teachings of the Pauline epistles, attracted large followers and mobilised the mass. This moving threat questioned religious war of Sainthood and played a critical role in the Independence of Zimbabwe, as it differed in approach but attracted large numbers despite classes hence thus it created a humanistic consciousness of the need to create non-racial society or racial inclusivity systems opposed to the colonial system. The eloquent interpretation of Holy Spirit, the power of Jesus, the demonstration of power, exorcism, miracles and prophecy mobilised ghettos, even those who believe in traditional religion. Pentecostal find place to grow, with large numbers and opened a lot of branches, depopulated European Christian established churches. In post-colonial Zimbabwe experiences these churches gain momentum in ghetto public space, people once exposed to Christianity by the Catholics, Anglicans and Protestant prepare the avenue to understand Pentecostal movement and seeking redemption from poverty that consume ghetto. The ghetto condition exposes them to this rising spirited religion. Apostolic Faith Mission (AFM), ZAOGA and various Faith Ministries are attended by thousands of people statistically. The increase in poverty and political crisis in Zimbabwe increased the call to worship and prayers as to deliver the people from incessant abject poverty. The most famous Pentecostal churches, moving from the pure doctrine of the early Pentecostal churches, UFIC led by former AFM pastor Immanuel Makandiwa rock the ghetto streets, its fame spread even across the country due to miracles and prophecy. Many people who have chronic diseases healed, the lame walk and people are delivered from abject poverty. The church attracts large followers, threaten even political parties. However Walter Magaya Prophetic Healing and Deliverance Ministries, Utawashe Family of God and various ministries rock the ghetto; mobilises millions of followers. Ghetto lived space, conquered by mass prayers, as to create a condition on how ghetto being relate to others and space, in so doing Pentecostalism also promotes mass mobilisation and is confirmed by history.

Prophet in Ghetto: A Redemptive Strategy

The Prophet is in the ghetto, exorcises anti-marriage spirits and delivers people from the demons. He is in the ghetto to proclaim the return to Jesus, as the saviour and the way. Proclaiming the doomsday as nearer showed by the signs of serious social pathological convictions. He is in the ghetto to conquer the ghetto space, with crusades and armis of youth singers inviting the crowd to church. He is in the ghetto to give people hope, preach about faith and prosperity. He is in the ghetto, demanding tithe and the blessed giver to extend their hands to the basket. People shouting Halleluiah! Shouting Amen!. Prophecy Papa! I Receive! The moment to believe of the role of Pentecostalism in delivering people from abject poverty, to gain momentum in contemporary politics, for people to think of generational cases as the causes of misfortunes and poverty. This kind of diagnosis, framed the topic of this section to confirm the relationship of Pentecostalism and redemption, on how it relates and meets? Is it the redemption of the soul? Or redeemed from the abject poverty? Mostly, ghetto prophet confirms both, but the astonishing part of it is that redemption from abject poverty is now the important theme. But with due respect, Ghetto prophet loudly call the people to the word of God, biblical ethics, such as the doctrine of love. Love as the central theme in every society, which manifest in form of sharing, charity and helping others, binds people together; it unites ghetto from its fragmentation outlook causeed by political hostilities prevailing in the country. Pentecostal redeems people from the growing ugly satanic world. But that form of redemption, redemption of the soul is questioned since ghetto prophet is accused of deceiving people, looting money from the poor ghetto people in the name of God and is involved in Scandalous Behaviour. So can it redeem people from poverty and sin, as its ideation systematic philosophy claims? And there are satanic allegations, whereby those prophets use charms from the dark world to perform miracles or even stage miracles. These allegations, though, there is little evidence, Pentecostalism is still the redemptive strategy in restoring the meaning of life. Ghetto condition left people desperate and easy prey to religious 'entrepreneurship'. In the earliest days, it manages to redeem people from colonialism as mass mobilisation strategy and the colonial interpretation of the Bible to support colonialism, it mobilises people and nourishes African nationalism. As a society, it replaces the ideal society which is raceless and classic and the true observers of ethics, towards a just and Saint Augustine 'City of God'. As peace activism, Pentecostalism calling for Christian principles in the ghetto space, is aimed at proclaiming the existentialism of Kantian-perpetual peace society, governed by reasoning as the man's highest faculty, embodied in the principle of harmony of the superiority of the soul over the body influenceing logical rationality. In post-colonial society it managed to redeem people from ugly world, exorcise demons, heal the sick and perform the miracles, but its prosperity gospel and ambitions disqualify its mandate to liberate people from abject poverty. Ghetto, as the highest concentration of the people is now a source of income of Ghetto Prophet, who becomes rich whilst the followers continue to languish in poverty. It is now a political game; transmogrify itself from justice as the founded principle to a more luxury and, material searching aspect. Albert Camus introduces the philosophy of absurdly, talking about suicide as abominable practice in religious believers and atheists, so life has values but to fight suicide it should have meaning. Ghetto life today has no meaning, yet Pentecostal came as source of solicit meaning to life.

Conclusion

Ghetto culture is not spared from religious activities, since the constructions of these urban residents, religion was the important element. In responding to ghetto condition, African's dungeons where the Wretched of the Earth nurse wounds of life caused by inflammation of colonialism, ghetto culture is premised on religion. Indigenous churches and Pentecostal movements play a most important role in liberation discourse, it is remembered that Africans were once referred to people without soul, but in search of full humanity with soul, mind and body, religious consciousness emanated, even today it is now difficult to say Africans are people without soul, because of massive religious existence in Africa, form even churches in Africa spreading out across the world. The search of ghetto being in Pentecostal space is based on the existentiality of hope, willingness to live and redemption. It is known that redemption from abject poverty and sin is a prerequisite of ghetto being.

Chapter 8
Streets of Revolution: Rethinking Women in Ghetto Public Space

Abstracts

Ghetto public space is a battle ground of struggles reflects in social, economic and political facets of life. As a space it provides freedom to the oppressed, it solicits an important social movement of contemporary world, the issue of feminism gain momentum as democratic human rights component is an important movement shaping the ghetto space. This guided philosophy, redefines post-humanistic world as it is more deconstructional and projected to dismantle the existing stereotypes and images of the society partly on woman. Ghetto streets, once a symbol of oppression is now a symbol of revolution and acts as a replica of Harlem renaissance in USA where Malcolm X, Marcus Garvey and Edward Blyden used to speak revolutionary speeches. Thousands of miles from Harlem Streets, Ghetto in Zimbabwe sow seeds of every form of revolution from pre-independence labour and civil rights movement to post-colonial feminists and youth movements. The main thrust of this paper is to scrutinise the position of women within ghetto culture and the objective is to emancipate women. Since it is embedded on subaltern uprisings, it means women are included as well; this is justified in women in politics, women in music. The phenomenology context of women, existence in ghetto space is of paramount importance in the construction of the philosophical thoughts of this paper, founded on Marxist feminism, liberal feminism and Africana womanism theoretical modes of analysis. Ghetto cosmology as liberation culture mostly founded its argument on Afrocentric consciousness to reclaim the Africa past; in this paper the author holds the opinion of Afro-centeredness woman movement as genuine discourse in establishing a post-colonial society.

Key Words, Streets, Public Space, Women

Introduction

Is there any space for women in ghetto? Who created that space? These questions inform theoretical contestations of this paper, since public space seems to condition women to conform to patriarchal ideologies and existing stereotypes, it is not neutrally and patriarchal constructed. It is of important consideration on the making of ghetto public space, in relation to women being in the present urban society, which give the impetus to the presentation of pragmatic arguments of this paper. Public space with no doubt is a man's construct, created to sustain the hierarchy systems based on sex and race. Sex is central in this discussion, a biological difference between man and woman, through social processes, it has been used as a normative discourse in constructing social systems whereby ghetto culture is informed in patriarchal lines. In this regard numerous arguments rises as social movement, can it be sulbaternizing the other subalterns? It focuses on emancipating the marginalised ghetto youth, but who are ghetto youth in gender perspective? If it is patriarchal how then will it be emancipatory culture? This paper seeks to explain ghetto-gender constructs tracing from colonial history, it also mandates to explain the theoretical basis of women emancipation according to ghetto culture and lastly questions the epistemology of ghetto culture, gender Zimdancehall and women in search of space in political trajectories.

Ghetto-Gender Construct: A Historical Analytics

In analysing the construction of ghetto space, how it becomes patriarchal, and why it's now a conducive space for women rights we will employ a historical analysis on the starting point of the problem, to the present and the deconstructionist project. Space is more important to define the existence of ghetto being, but this section is themed at giving the relationship between women as subaltern being and ghetto space as a colonial-patriarchal construct. Of course the relationship might be dialectical, either it conforms or its in rebellion, hence more confirmation in hypothetical development lies in history. The objective of colonialism, go beyond even to colonised social space, whereby it was fed by the alien culture to Africans (Diop 1974 and Mazrui 1986), but before colonial history, an important event on this subject cannot be forgotten in the construction of women as male subjects. After the Fall of Granada, Valladolid judgement claims that black people are people without soul, hence it was not actually a sin to enslave them since there are closer to animals, though a little bit intelligence than animals. The claim was sustained by the writings of Fredric Hegel, which also popularised the notion of Africans as people without history. This judgement, unleashed an army of the so called Saints, priest to convert Africans from the animalistic spiritual practises to Christianity, since they were referred to as non-beings but needed Salvation from the word of God. Though it is communicated as the mission civilistrice, but the agenda was to colonise the continent, demonise African religions since they acted as a source of pride and identity. It acted as vehicle in the construction of ghetto condition, though oppression of blacks, it went on to annihilate their way of life and reduced the role of women in public space. Pre-colonial public sphere designed in an inclusive system, whereby "I am because I belong" discourse provided testimonial evidence to the existentiality of non-patriarchal Africa's past. Contrary to this, European culture was entrenched in Judeo-Christian tradition patriarchal norms, was presaged the ideal society, spread to colonies as a social system. The fall of Granada as the most important event (Grosfoguel 2007), explained in the position of women philosophers murdered and burnt alive, accused of witchcraft but the main reason was to destroy threat and embellish the power of Catholic cultures. European society as historically shaped by patriarchal culture, replaced the inclusive-pluralistic African way of life, marked the genesis of disappearing of women in public spaces. The report of Lord Macaulay to British Parliament, evidenced the strength of African culture, but proposing a plan to replace it as political control strategy, followed by the development of urban settlement as easy way to spread European cultures. The development of urban culture, mostly man migrated from the rural reserves in search of employment to fend for the family- the discourse of power relation constructed shifted from traditionally-pluralistic society to a more hierarchical society entrenched in patriarchy. Apart from power relations discourse, as a result of creation of ghettos, ghetto condition premised on Judeo-Christianity tradition deny women ontology in public sphere as dictated by the doctrines of Sainthood in Christian Churches. This mode of culture relegated woman to the periphery, and constructed images and stereotypes about women as lesser beings. Education system, coloniality of knowledges stretches to the animated thought on absence of women in knowledge, since there were denied existence in philosophy; once discovered as intellectual they were being killed or burnt alive after the Fall of Granada, in Iberian Peninsula. Most of the Indian women scholars suffered the same fate; hence there was no prominent women philosopher in physical science, political science, philosophy and sociology. This system of education sustain European colonialism, not just of space or time but of women, since it created the imaginary discourse of African inferiority interims of knowledge production rested on Rene Descartes philosophy of "I think, therefore I am", an individual mode of being (Mignolo 2013). It also destroyed the African unity through entrenching superior-inferior dichotomy based on sex. The formation of knowledge and cosmologies were built on inclusivity, the removal of women as thinking beings, casted down as objects and subjects to existing norms and powerless being, resulted in the collapse of African culture. This ghetto condition, though it oppressed blacks, but woman suffered double barrelled situation, of being black in the world and being women in the world. Women modes of being, especially women of colour narratives are written by bloody tears since the suffering were totally unbearable. The existence of Zimbabwe history, history of nationalism was not deliberately constructed the way it is in narratives and literature, patriarchal historiography but due to ghetto condition (Gaidzanwa 1985); ghetto culture become even more patriarchal since public space were for man, woman were not available, relegated to kitchen duties and even to rural areas. Prominent figures such as Joshua Nkomo, Edgar Tekere, Robert Mugabe and Ndabanhingi Sithole as products of ghetto are the most celebrated nationalist and there is no any woman on the list who matches the character on this man's role in liberation struggle, because of the space, which was too patriarchal, originating from the cultures of Vatican City. This system provides a foundation of ghetto culture, which is largely male dominated, but new social diagnosis provides measures on deconstructionist and decolonial projects in the dichotomy of emancipation-liberation movements. The space is of critical importance in the existence of being, as historically presented, woman bodies exist in ghetto public sphere but relevance in that space were so limited, which even led to the adoption of various woman empowerment conventions to promote the existentiality of woman as being, a powerful being to contribute to social thoughts. Ghetto as the conducive environment of every revolution also paves the way for woman emancipatory project.

Theoretical Basis of Woman Emancipation; Women According to Ghetto

Ghetto as the lived space, awards abject poverty to the residents it is by no means an area of intellectual development in providing a critical solution to the problem. Analysis of women colonial and post-colonial ghetto space, not contrasting but builds a hypothesis of these two different times and creates a critical comprehension of the position today, but theoretical designs cannot be ignored. This section employ feminist theories to construct the critical thoughts, but before this a prologue might create a meaning statue of the arguments. The post-colonial ghetto founded on the principles of human liberty opposes to the colonial situation, and a phase explains the death end of colonialism, though there are tangible contestation thoughts about the existence of this phase in Africa (Adiche 2006 and 2014). Though post-colonial existence is debated, but the construction of the episodes is still in progress, on the basis of struggle to emancipate woman. Remembering Thomas Sankara, he once said, "Social liberation is meaningless without woman liberation". From these golden words, it means the role of Africa's social liberation, must be defined at the same time with woman emancipation, to make sense the meaning of post-coloniality. Thomas Sankara thought reflects a cosmos past, with no inferiors whereby Burkina Faso was constructed on the great history of the Mossi people, and mossi queens who were army generals and rulers. It technically means African past was not patriarchal at all. The theoretical propositions for women freedoms is limited since is employs emancipation as the modus operandi in dismantling patriarchy, but Thomas Sankara made it clear that there is need for liberation as a total project for liberties. Taking into consideration, liberal feminism challenge to the structure of public sphere which excludes women in governance and public sphere but maintains social values (Adichie 2014, Gaidzanwa 2000). Mary Astell and Mary Wollstonecraft propagate the philosophical movement of woman liberties, relating liberal feminism to ghetto culture, its nature of questioning the existing cultural norms of politics conceived educated and women politicians who represented women voices in public spheres. The role of women is being recognised, rooted from governance style of liberal feminism (Adichie 2014). However, ghetto people are labour capital residents, the dialectical materialism devolved to black and blacks, whereby means of production remains the source of division; created the inferior-superior relations between male and female, hence bred gender violence. In dealing with this situation, ghetto culture as the emancipatory-liberatory system, women societies and unions formed to challenge the issue of income inequality as the source of subjugation and increase the social power of women in the ghetto space. A revolution championed by unions through established human rights laws informed by Convention of Elimination of All Forms of Discrimination Against Women (CEDAW) of 1948 and SADC Gender Protocol cleans ghetto space for social and political involvement of women in the reflection of ghetto experience. In addition, the construction of theoretical proposition towards women emancipation is fighting the structure, institutions and system that are artificial. Adichie (2014) states that, people create cultures, there are artificial and those cultural structures imprisons the other, of not blacks its women in the lived-space, hence fighting racism is also at the same time a human rights projects for woman of colour. Post-modern feminism (Butler 2004, Lugones 2003 and Connell 2012) is about fighting the existing social, epistemology and cultural structures which make women as subjects, inferior and in most cases objects. In the liberation struggle, post-modern feminism based on deconstructionist project channelled through the liberation movement, for instance Winnie Mandela (Ndhlovu-Gatsheni 2015) as a women of colour, from the ghetto of Soweto she bravely blend woman and socialist activism to liberate the subalterns in apartheid South Africa. The struggle continues in Zimbabwe ghettos, whereby post-colonial feminist writers also blame racism as a fascist ideology aimed to dehumanise people of the south. Harlem Renaissance, various Afrocentric feminism movements projected on the condition of women of colour, who have been victimized through slavery and other social injustices. In analysis, the discourse of liberty remains the central issue of ghetto culture in search of Zimbabwe in post-colonial society as post-humanist project.

Epistemology of Ghetto Culture, Afrocentric and Gender

"I believe blacks were oppressed by white: female by male: peasant by landlords: and workers by lord of capital. It follows from this that the black female worker and peasant is the most oppressed. She is oppressed on account of her colour like all black people in the world: and she is oppressed on account of her gender like all woman in the world: and she is exploited and oppressed on account of her class like all workers and peasants in the world. Three burdens she has to carry" (Wa Thiongo 2007)

Ngugi wa Thiongo clarifies the discourse of woman oppression, woman of the south; hence ghetto feminism must be at the same time workers revolution, fighting against racism and patriarchal cultures. That is to say, its objectives are in the human liberation movements. Feminism in ghetto culture must be Afrocentric at the same time embrace African agency in its liberationist praxis. The problem with contemporary global south is coloniality of the mind, but in liberation struggle the project was largely political than going deeper into catastrophic confusion of colonization (Asante 2007). Mkandawire (2010) groups African scholars into four generations, whereby all generations focuses on Afro-Marxist interpretation of the impacts of colonialism to Africa, referencing the issue of exploitation, dependency and the creation of economic world order which relegates Africa to the margins, but though Ngugi wa Thiongo, Kwasi Wiredu, Cheikh Anta Diop just to mention a few diagnose the mental effects of colonialism and global structure, the interpretation of concepts are still being cantered on the Euro-American world. The increase in decolonial scholarship is much celebrated because of its informative discourse of aiding the epistemic restorative agenda of the continent (Maldonado-Toress 2016), through Fanon (1967) and Biko (1970s) observations, designs and proposed methods. Ghetto cosmology, the discourse of gender is a critical issue, whereby as a Eurocentric construct and infested with 'double consciousness' problematize the ghetto space in its failure to define women and man in African thought-system (Haundonji 2010). Feminism movements remain a source of social confusions, though human rights projects in the sense that it treats woman as direct enemies of man, divide the world into two camps and deny the harmony existence of the society. This argument is not to say feminism is, but its Eurocentric design is not fit to the African communities, since the world is not a single universe, but a construct of universes. Huntington (1996) admits that, universalising Pax America (American culture) destabilised global initiatives towards peace in post-cold war reconstruction, various civilizations struggled to search space, hence frictions or civilisation clashes explode into serious lethal wars, or serious social conditions led to the demise of different societies. In doing so, the issue of women is universal, but different cultures have different methodologies. In Jamaican ghettos, the nation of God and Earth symbolises a feminist movement which recognises the social harmony, labelling man as the highest being and women as the Earth, provides life and lived space in philosophy and social relations. Dona Haraway (2013), Mazama (2003) and Hudson (2004) Afrocentric womanist, based on the paradigm of African Agency in woman struggle acts in contrary with western feminism theories denying the African values as source of social stability, but it is a sorry case to acknowledge the failure of feminisms, gender activism and women movements failure to acknowledge coloniality of being. This catastrophic confusion threatens both the movement and society.

> "I do not blame black men, what I'm saying is, we have to take a new look at ways in which we fight our joint oppression because If we don't we're going to be blowing each other up. We have to begin to redefine the terms of what woman is, what man is, how we relate to each other" (Baldwin 1960)

James Baldwin, a product of Harlem renaissance once questioned the position of man and woman whereby the existing sociology failed to give a comprehensive method of constructing the so-called equal society, since the existing methods are more toxic to social relations and collective values as people. This is evidenced in the increase of the divorces in urban areas putting children into disgrace. It does not mean the paper is anti-feminist, but is aimed at mapping the contours of decolonial feminism, gender and to create a well-defined equal society.

> "Gender is a colonial imposition, not just that it imposes itself on life as lived in tune with cosmology incompatible with the modern logic of dichotomies, but also that inhabitants of the world understood, constructed and in accordance with such cosmologies animated the self-among-others in resistance from and at the extreme tension of the colonial differences" (Oyewini 1997)

Modernity organises and construct gender ontology in terms of space categories of man and woman, opposing the Afrocentric Ma'at principle of harmony. The post-colonial approaches to social change manages to create the need to decolonise feminism as component from critical thinking point of view (Mendiza 2006, Ballerstrin 2006). Assessing the application of gender discourses to the global south, its forms of epistemology and a gender equality society informs the standpoint of decolonial feminism Ghetto culture and provides space for woman in music, not just only woman oriented music such as gospel but Zimdancehall whereby Lady Squander, Ninja Lips, Darula to mention a few challenge the existing status quo and dominate in the genre. In most cases ghetto culture as the response to colonialism, coloniality and post-colonial political oppression; the question of woman rights is also in the lenses, embedded on the cultural artefacts of African cosmology.

Conclusion

The discourse of woman is the most contested idea in political sphere, whereby the gender equality movement developed to emancipates woman. As the streets of revolution, ghetto culture facilitates the existence of woman in public sphere. Through music and arts women are seen participating in the forefront of ghetto public sphere. These developments are also evidenced in women football, woman league and the rise of women representation groups. Though Eurocentric gender discourses pillage ghetto stability, its also noted that, Afrocentric must take a centre stage to redefine man and woman not to compromise social relations.

Chapter 9
Music in Post-Colonial Ghetto: Winky D Decolonial Thoughts in Njema Song

Abstract

Ghetto being exists as a result of the presence of ghetto space as metaphysics, experiences and aspiration in the boarders of ghetto residents and conditions. This phenomenology context formulates the critical argument of this paper, tracing the ghetto lived-space and existentiality as others, as explained in this book, music invented to create relevance, assurance and answer to the existentiality of being in the society. Winky D known as Wallace Chimukiro is a decorated Zimdancehall songwriter, singer and performer mostly singing about ghetto culture, singing within. He is a post-colonial music icon, a ghetto product playing a critical role to ghetto's mutual understanding of oneness and revolution through music. Music unites all ghetto youth beyond ghetto political boundaries. The thrust of this essay is to explore the decolonial message in Winky D song Njema, as the commitments towards the creation of post-colonial Zimbabwe and social transformation.

Key Words, Zimdancehall, Ghetto, Njema

Introduction

The struggle for creating post-colonial Zimbabwe continues in the post-independence epoch since the power transformation from the white colonialist celebrated as the discontinuity of colonialism but failed to see the continuities of the systems. In this regard, the present social and political systems evidenced the existence of coloniality of power in the so called post-independence. Fanon (1963) warned the continent about the negativity of African nationalism, as projected by petty bourgeoisies which is much more alienated to the African values and become leaders. As a result, the much anticipated political hopes vanish demonstrated by the existence of political fascism, brutalities and gross violation of human rights similar to that of colonial era. The bourgeois were alienated to African values, it means they were alienated to African people as well as brutalities became a much prioritised method to crush rebellions and establish social order. In doing so, music came as journalistic attempts to criticise governments, the post-colonial, and Chimurenga music remained attached to the values of the past and campaigned on the establishment of true leadership. Youth in ghetto also used music to communicate their story, ideas and aspirations as anti-marginalisation movement. This paper is aimed at exploring the role of music in ghetto being and how it express the situation of mental slavery in post-colonial society. The paper is divided into three, music as theory of social consciousness, political landscape and music and Winky D decolonial credence in Njema

.

Music, Culture and Ghetto Space: Theory of Social Consciousness

From psychology point of view, the psychodynamic theory made it clear that the social relations of individual being is much projected in superego or developed moral space. This moral space provides a learning environment of certain modes of behaviours as exposed to different experiences and situations. In ghetto society, the living conditions provide a learning idea of hustling and revolutionary cultures as the aspiration though which to escape the condition. Music becomes one of the most important issues in the modern politics aid social consciousness, and explains the shared mutual knowledge about social realities and methods to escape it. The ghetto condition is more frustrated whereby social life is more suicidal and absurd as it is explained by Camu, since methods to escape sometimes failed, in most cases it failed to materialise and ghetto become the life style and lived space. Social consciousness continues to rule the mentality, but music is of profound importance to stimulate revolution. Ghetto songs served three major purposes, namely documentation of ghetto life, diversion from reality and upholding tradition. It reveals the capacity for suffering and the elemental will to survive and the urge to create, to sing or even laugh. As a result of poor conditions it helps the ghetto being to divert from the existing reality and promotes the traditions. For Kindsley (2019), the Zimbabwe story is narrated through Zimdancehall lyrics, especially ghetto conditions whereby Killer T sing the song "Ghetto rinenharo" (The strength of ghetto) narrating ghetto life and the means of survival in this economic hardships. Music culture facilitates social consciousness.

Post-Colonial Zimbabwe Landscape and Ghetto Experience

The party fought for liberation of its people, turned its wrath against the people (Salih 2003); it was once a people's party, won liberation war because of the people and once a people's oriented party, it divert from its commitment around 1990s as a result of growing popular discontent, polarity of the party due to corruption and the adoption of Economic Structural Adjustment Programme (ESAP).

ESAP adopted by Finance Minister Dr Bernard Chidzero a Harvard Scholar, bringing untold misery to Zimbabwe since it was implemented through devaluation of the currency, deregulation of industries that is to say privatisation and democratisation (Raftopolous 2000, Sachikonye 2011 and 2012). The government drifted away from its socialist policy and adopted a capitalist model of government which brings serious crisis, increased unemployment and the suffering of the blacks. As a result, Movement for Democratic Change (MDC) headed by the late Morgan Richard Tsvangirai as a labour party formed from Zimbabwe Congress of Trade Union (ZCTU) received popular support and threatened the position of the ZANU PF. The government embarked on land reform programme aimed at empowering blacks (Muchemwa 2013) as a Pan African redemptive strategy, since land is used as heritage, a source of dignity, food and above all identity. This historical correction, as anti-imperialist agenda led to the imposition of sanctions and the economy continued to bleed. In this regard, MDC was blamed for sanctions, beings neo-colonialist project and regime change agenda. Post-colonial music criticises the government system of corruption. Thomas Mapfumo music on "Corruption" and "Mamvemve" narrates post-colonial tragedies whereby petty bourgeoisies as was warned by Fanon (1963) begin to suffice, politicians embezzling funds for themselves and failing to run the government, characterised by poor service delivery. Leonard Zhakata in his song "Mugove" demonstrated how capitalistic labour exploitation problematizes the creation of post-colonial Zimbabwe. The question, Why the country once referred to as the bread basket of Africa collapsed? Academias try to answer it by initiating prelude the House of Hunger and Democratic Debate at SAPES however musicians also conceptualise it through music so as to spread message even to the margins. Post-colonial ghetto music address four distinct themes, hunger, corrupt administration, the hope for freedom and a call for revolt. Kinsley (2019) argued that a number of musicians are now discontented with the Mnangagwa administration part, a more widespread disillusionment with the post-Mugabe transition. It rails on the situation of alleged rigged elections, the August 1 2018 killings and torture of the civilians by the army, and January 2019 raids by the army in ghetto residents. Poptain, a rising Zimdancehall star sings "All I wanted was freedom, instead we are getting free doom", in this regard, the question of freedoms as post-colonial anticipated values is still closed in the mantle of political violence whereby instead of having freedoms, people are tortured, alleged cases of abduction and the cat and mouse system of the city of Harare and the vendors, described as *vendorphobia*. The increase in unemployed graduates led to the imminent rise of vending as a way for survival, and because of their numbers the legal sites are not enough, some of them begin to sell their products at illegal spaces and faced the wrath of city council, therefore vendorphobia is also a theme in post-colonial ghetto songs to defend them from the incompetency government that failed to resuscitate economy as a result of corruption and political repression. Government's decision to unleash the army received widespread condemnation from musicians, Tockey Vybes also sing about it in his song "Zvirinani", reminding the army to fight for the people against the repressive system rather than to defend it through wiping and killing the unarmed civilians. However, Kufakurinani and Mwatwara (2017) conceptualises ghetto voices as forms of violence, youth subculture fitted into violence but the main cause of it was the increase in youth bulge and unemployed graduates, their voices are not a form of violence as these two authors declare but voices of the voiceless, negotiating space and informing the relevant authority about 'ghetto youth' marginalisation. Kufakurinani and Mwatwara (2017) use the analogue analysis of Arab Spring, whereby the ghetto subcultures manifest into violence which swept away authoritarian governments in Tunisia and Egypt in 2011. This is different to the present ghetto condition in Zimbabwe, though youth turn to be more liberal and a little bit lawlessness, there are caged by music since it helps them to document hardship, escape reality and also communicate the rage to the masses. The availability of recording studios such as Chillspot promotes the ghetto culture of music to spread quickly, those songs cover a wide range of themes of social experiences such as politics, love, economics and entertainment. Enzo I shall is a product of Chiilspot, and his hit songs "Kanjiva" helps ghetto youth to escape reality, since it was more entertaining and clearly shows the existence of talents in ghetto. In this regard, ghetto youth are aware of the present political environment and ghetto cosmology as emancipatory ideology, aimed at dismantling this situation politically, through democratic project.

Winky D-Decolonial Thoughts in Njema Song

The post-colonial society introduces new struggles. Ghetto youth struggle for relevance and survival is the serious economic crisis condition, which later breeds social pathology in form of 'hwindi' hustlers, criminals and the Jamaican rooted Zimdancehall as means of communicating the music. Winky D, originally known as Wallace Chirumiko born on 31 January 1983 rose in music in 2005, as ghetto-dancehall pioneers digressing from the existing urban groove. Winky D produced a number of hit albums including Pakitchen (2011), Gafa Futi (2016), Gafa Life Kicks Tape, Gombwe: Chiextra (2018), Njema 2020. The music icon is defined as a voice of the voiceless since his lyrical contents though it express deep art and poetry, also comments on the political situation of Zimbabwe, his song 'copyrights" commented by Mazingaidzo (2019) as political since it narrates the difficulties of the realities of Zimbabwe situation, by saying *"tisu tine macopyrights enhamo, tinongoseka sengano"*, in translation "We own poverty, and we believe it's not real". It's a lyrical expression of what is happening in Zimbabwe, and people are engaged in survival strategies to make poverty just an illusion. He is the voice of voiceless, representing the ordinary ghetto Zimbabweans.

"Winky D music is also satirical. The singer speaks on behalf of the ordinary and lampoons the failures of the leadership and their excesses, which are responsible for the society's impoverishment. One of the lyrical personae in 'Survivor' presents a crude caricature of the city canal excesses and vendorphobia. He draws on the imaginary of demons where he presents the city council as demon possessed and imagines the evictions of the helpless venders where he presents the city council as demonic for the government has not come up with viable solutions to the lack of employment opportunities for the people" (Tivenga 2018)

From this lyrical analysis, Tivenga (2018) justifies Winky D as a voice of the voiceless, speaking on behalf of the misery of unemployed youth, helpless venders, ghetto youth and the ordinary people over the prevailing political situation emanated from bad leadership, a fascist-nationalist regime aimed to enrich the top echelons and make the masses suffer. It is a form of capitalist government, whereby the politicians as rich-tycoons continued to subvert existing rules for their personal gains (Vambe 2008, Sachikonye 2015). This leadership crisis emanated from the coloniality of being, since at the eve of the independence nationalist leaders were most alienated people to the roots of the cultures and assumed leadership positions, described in Fanon (1967) as petty bourgeoisie and therefore fitted Malcom X description of House Negro, totally brainwashed. The post-colonial Marxist politics hijacked by the neo-capitalist, the so called war veteran discourse though a preservation of the historical legacy, but it problematize the concept of leadership in Zimbabwe, hence musicians expose this to the society. Tivenga (2018) also introduces the discourse of demon possessed councils as expressed by Winky D, it is true that the City Council is demon possessed, possessed with demons of poor governance, commits corruption, failing to provide service delivery yet witchhunts vendors who are victims of the same corruption, who also search for a living. It is so sad, so painful and fascistic; this is what Mandani (2010) analyzes by saying, this is the world we least prepared for, and Mazrui (1986) put it in this way- the rulers begun to rule with crudest sense and the masses reduced to hungry sycophants praises and Ayittey (1999) described it as the transmogrification of dreams of development into melodramic nightmare. In this regard, musicians who challenges this are against what Grosfoguel (2019) analysis of the problem of continuities in discontinuities, since the repressive system continues, blacks are still trapped in the snare of colonial structures of government, hence it presents decolonial thoughts in the lyrical content to challenge the present government's activities. Winky D qualifies to be a decolonial scholar together with Jah Prayzah (Mukudzei Mukombe), joining the alumni of great musicians such as Bob Marley, Fela Kuti, Hugh Masekela, Oliver Mtukudzi, Thomas Mapfumo just to mention a few in challenging the existing culture of racism originated during the time of trans-atlantics slave trade and colonialism. In his album Njema, it portrays the call for creating a post-colonial being, oriented to the cultural glory and fight what the Harlem Renaissance and Afro-American Studies call mental slavery (Cress Welsing 1994, Ani 1994, Asante 2007, Clarke 1998), since our bodies are claimed to be free but our minds are still chained. Njema Album also has the fascinating song Ijipita, which is a satirical to the present political situation referencing the Exodus of Israelis from Egypt, giving hope of the future and the will to live as a ghetto being in ghetto space. The song Ijipita is also similar to "disappear" as diversion from reality, a psychotherapy that divert the attention of the people from the existing crises to cling onto hope not as allusion but a reality to unfold in the future.

Njema Songs: Lyrical Discourse Analysis

> Dzakambotanga dzakakaka nyama (We were physically chained)
> Iko zvino dzokakata pfungwa (Mental Slavery)
> Mukukura ndaingoti munyama (All though growing up it was misfortunes all along)
> Zvondirwadza pandinozvifunga (It's so painful when it rings in my mind)

In this regard this lyrical content qualifies Winky D art as decolonial music, since it introduces the idea of mental slavery, where Bob Marley warn global South to emancipate from mental slavery. He presents in accurately from how it originated, as transatlantic slave trade whereby Africans were shipped to America for forced labour and later colonialism was sustained. Ngugi wa Thiongo (2010) states that,

"Berlin Conference of 1884 was affected through sword and the bullets. But the night of sword and the bullet was followed by the morning of the chalk and blackboard. The physical violence of classroom" (wa Thiongo 2014)

In this regard it conceptualises Ngugi wa Thiongo and Winky D's position, the history of the present complex coloniality evolved first as physical slavery, and now presage in mental slavery manifesting in a form self-hate, it was projected by the religious brainwashing, demonization of culture and epistemicide. Mental slavery is blamed for the post-colonial confusion in nation building, and ghetto being alienated to the past and trapped in the snare of mental slavery.

Ndaisifunga Kuti zvoni vasungwa Ndivo vari muchizarira (I thought prisoners are only those in prisons)
Kusaziva kuti hobho vasungwa Vari panze vari kuzvifarira (I failed to recognise that, real prisoners are in the society)
Vachipika mutongo vari panze Kusungwa kwefunga hatizvivanze (Serving jail terms outside prison, truly mental slavery)

Tobata chipi chingatinyaradze Hanzi kufunga kwedu ngakutiparadze (Nothing can console us, because our way of thinking destroys the social fabrics)
Chiraramo chofundwa pazvi vhiti vhiti, Taane ruvengo takungorwisana sama dzviti (Learning through tv media which represents the European superiority, self-hate manifest in war of all against all)
Akaendepi magungano ataiwonesana chiraramo nemitambo yejiti (We losts our cultural values, where we learn about life and the relfections of life)

Winky D's lyrical contents explained above uses a post-structuralism theory and traditional decolonial thought, since from post-structural point of Michael Foucault (1963) in the "Birth of Prison" he argued that, real prisons are the social conditions created for social controls and limits human freedoms, these conditions also chained the mind, conditioned it as an object to think in a certain way. Africans are walking prisoners, ghetto youths are walking prisoners, since there are mentally enslaved, whereby universities, institutions and social space are trapped in the snares of coloniality, hence Africans always feel inferior to the whites and it shows the manifestation of mental slavery. The universalisation of Imperial Being and the contemporary project of mental slavery is facilitated through media, whereby the discourse of self-hate begun since the media content glorifies the Eurocentric way of life, Eurocentric way of thinking and African aesthetics are demonised. The Hollywood culture demonises the cultural aesthetic of people of the south; continues the project of superior-inferior global sociological structure (Maldonado-Tores 2010). The issue of civil wars resulted from mental slavery; since the horrific Rwandan genocide of 1994, Xenophobia in South Africa and the ceaseless conflicts in Congo are conditioned into African ghettos to establish a total control to the rich resource areas. It goes that way, the collapse of Ubuntu cultural values is based on deep kinships or social relations that emphasises the importance of community and neighbourhood, replaced by the Cartesian Individuation modes of being created a narcissist thinking and breed violence and conflicts. It's all because of mental slavery, since one used to care for the community and social relations in ghetto, but in contemporary times only one cares for his or her own selfish gains which resulted in serious conflicts. In this regard, the social histories of Zimbabwe in diaspora, in South Africa who fled from the post-colonial ghetto conditions are facing xenophobic attacks, but its roots are mental slavery projected by the colonialism and media in the present society. Blacks are referred to as barbaric but that barbarism is sourced from mental slavery.

Verse 3]
Zvatinoshuwira kuita nemoyo Zvese zvinonofira mupfungwa (Our thoughts never surface)
Mupfungwa mune hondo sepaChimoio, Ndimo mune chigaro chehusungwa (Our minds are at war like at Chimoio, house of the crown of imprisonment)
Chakatirera tachitanangira, Hatichagone kuti tichiteere (We forget our past and we can't listen to our values anymore)
Ndamboti ndizame kutsanangura, Ndiri kupa mashoko mbeveve (I tried to explain it but no one is in a position to understand it)

Tavakuronda tsika dzechingere, Matare achapihwa nani kupwere (We are Europeanised, who is going to taught us values)
Vari pasi tinokumbirawo nzeve, Tibviseiwo zvakakaka njere (Plea to the ancestors, help us to deconstruct mental slavery, to unchain our minds)

In this lyrical presentation the musician made it clear that post-colonial mental confusion resulted from mental slavery which erodes confidence to walk the talk, or to relate African cognitive ability with the practical world. For instance, in the current tertiary education set-up there is huge gulf between learning and social realities problematizing the post-colonial national building, since the learned theories across all disciplines are highly theoretical and the curriculum was designed to create labourers, not thinkers, the situation continues in post-colonial university up to now the recent education 5.0 policy launched to decolonise epistemologies across all discipline as heritage approach oriented policy. The battle of the minds represent schizophrenic confusion of identity, the relations of the body and the mind, conditioned to act in certain behaviours whereby Dibash (2013) ask the question, Can Non-Europeans think? Since the epistemologies are from the Euro-American world it conditions Africans ghetto being to remain in periphery. The relationship between ghetto being and the past is presented in the lyrical content, since the past is a source of foundation and values but contemporary ghetto being brainwashed is failing to relate to the past. That is how mental slavery become effective, it first erased the memory of the past to Africans presented as people without historical conscience and the glory of Ancient Egypt and other heritage sites was removed from African history and presented as part of the Mediterranean civilisation. Diop (1974), Sertima (2002), Asante (2000) and Clarke (1998) reclaims African history through historical projects presenting the early presence of Africans in America before Christopher Columbus claims of discovery, black pedigree of Egyptian civilization and Africa as the cradle of all civilisations. This is aimed at restoring confidence and manufacture black superiority, emanated from Harlem Renaissance of Marcus Garvey words which state that "Black is not a badge of shame but symbol of superiority".

> "To control a people you must first control what they think about themselves and how they regard as the history and culture. And when your conqueror makes you ashamed of your culture and your history, he needs no prison walls and no chains to hold you" (Clarke 1998)

John Henrick Clarke made it clear, to control a people their history must be erased and dislocate them from their past. This simply in the lyrics of Njema song, as viewing the past as the dark history which simply means ghetto being, or ghetto youth are just people who are vulnerable and easily controlled by the western propaganda since they are like trees without roots, they do not know or sterilised their affection with the past, which means it is now difficult to remember the dismembered cultural values. The future of the continent is predictably a total social apocalypses, since the lyrics made it clear that contemporary society view decolonial thought as nonsense, since there are Europeanised. For Kapuya (2019), the Europeanisation of Africans referred to the creation of the ontology of the other whereby Africans are alienated from their cultural foundation to

116

emulate Europeans, but because of skin colour they cannot be European enough, and yet become non-Africans, hence ontology of the other, so the future of ghetto being is predictably a disaster. Winky D pleads to the ancestors to decolonise the mental slavery, it demonstrates the musician's knowledge of Afrocentric theory of social change symbolised by the bird Sankofa aimed at remembering the dismembered, the once demonised ancestral ritualism projects the way forward to help the bewitched ghetto being mind. It's not just anti-progressive perspective, but a decolonial tradition informed by the past glory for the future social blueprints, since as it is, it is a self-prophecy of social disaster. The process to unchain the minds is relating to the historical recognitions and the existence of cultural values, whereby the musician and the author agree with Nabudere (2013) Afrikology as a template of knowledge embraces the art of knowing the cultures and rituals of African people. Though urban-residents are the most alienated people but the possibility of relating to the past historiography aids the process of unchaining the mind, as well as decolonise the Europeanised institutions. Winky D communicates with every one, and the ordinary citizens since the lyrics are performed in widely spoken language across all ghettos.

Conclusion

Post-colonial ghetto music at first as urban grooves was more western, mainly themed on love songs, but Zimdancehall came forcefully and expressed the ghetto conditions, speaking on the marginalising of people and act as source of psychological entertainment because of its hard, fast theatre performance. It covers the issue of politics as the major trending issue in post-colonial

Zimbabwe, showing discontent to the present governance system. The issue of poverty, unemployment and vendorphobia influence the lyrical existence of political criticism, Winky D as the voice of the voiceless, a voice of helpless vendors, voice of ghetto youth, voice of political victims in post-colonial Zimbabwe through music, also goes beyond and joins the decolonial stoicism. He aimed at creating a true post-colonial ghetto through Njema music that contains deep lyrical discourses to present the issue of mental slavery, ghetto being and coloniality space and as well as decolonial paradigm which creates a possible better future society. In this regard, decoloniality is not just a mere theory, but premised on social theory to create confidence in the blacks, declared inferior by the white race.

Chapter 10
The Betrayal to Post-Colonial Ghetto Cosmology: Crimes, Identity Crisis, Self-hate and Beyond

Abstract

G hetto culture is a social invention existing because of social interactions which creates values in a lived space responding to the realities of the ghetto society. These values exist in the borders of the dichotomy of positive-negative but mainly engrossed in the subjectivity of the society, it is not universal and somehow applicable just for a specific time frame. The main thrust of this paper is to explore the dynamics of ethics in post-colonial ghetto resulting from the perpetuity of drifting away from well-established human values emanated from Ma'at dubbed as Ubuntu. This collapse, in most cases is the Achilles heel of ghetto cosmology which betrays its own objective in liberating ghetto being from the 'imposed social conditions, thinking and political marginalisation of the youth'. It is more inspired by drug abuse, criminal activities and perilous self-hatred originated from the coloniality complex of the world. In an attempt to rescue ghetto being from 'blackness' as a savagery norm, backward and primitive as anti-decolonialist claim, it resulted in serious self-hate which eventually bore social pathologies. In this regard, the ghetto youth movement is reduced to nothing, useless and just a schizophrenic behaviour. This paper interrogates further the discourse of criminal psychology in interpreting the causes of crimes in ghetto to provide a critical solution on facilitating the recognition of ghetto renaissance in post-colonial Zimbabwe. It is argued that as ghetto founded on the detribalised society, once deprived of rights to practise African cultures which were declared barbaric, dark arts in Judeo-Christian tradition manifests in form of poor ethical values among ghetto youth. In Harlem ghetto and Jamaican ghettos, drug trafficking continues to dehumanize those societies, disown them from ethical values which compromise revolution. It is far much tangible to engage in the sociotherapy in re-introducing the lost cultural ethics in mapping the contours of genuine 'ghetto cosmology'.

Key Words; Drugs, Ethics, Crimes, Vulgar

Introduction

The increase in crimes, drug abuse and meta-existence of vulgarity betrays ghetto cosmology, threatens its mission, existence and remain the major weakness. It is reduced to nothing, meaningless movement and self-conflicting culture. However, the source of these social ills need to be clarified since no conclusion cannot be arrived without contextualising psychological effects of colonialism to ghetto being, how it transforms from an ideological-event to a system. The paper aimed at establishing the transcendental thoughts in the relationship between subject and object as the foundation of existentiality in the lances of criminal psychology. In most cases, it is unjust to solely blame on coloniality, though it did much damage in demonizing the cultural values of people of the South, human nature and poor governance also plays a part. Ghetto streets are bleeding, once washed clean by the blood of the martyrs in liberation struggle, but the gains of it is still illusory of the contemporary ghetto streets, crimes defines the order of the day. This paper is divided into three broad sections, aimed at exploring the uncharted areas of knowledge in ghetto and crime, the author aimed at contributing to existing debate about crimes and drug abuse in post-colonial ghetto.

The Psychological Being; Experiences and Crimes: Ghetto Survey

Criminal psychologist seeks to provide answers on the complex questions such as, why an individual commits crimes. Why crimes present in our society. Criminal psychology provides answers, though subjects to debates due to massive research and available of literature largely contrasting each other on the similar subject, but psychological position provides satisfactory answers due to its explanation of the relationship of the mind and body, the mind and human behaviours. In the context of ghetto, crimes are committed to highest degree which degrades ghetto cosmology liberation project. The main weakness of ghetto liberation project is that it is not immune from crimes, ghetto condition itself it is an absurd environment which more or less contributed to the criminal situation of the place, ranging from theft, homicide, murder and robbery. In Zimbabwe, the concept *Matsotsi* is applied to urban settlers, involved in criminal activities and it is a betrayal to ghetto cosmology, a manifestation of self-hate and confusion. It is believed that Mbare housed a lot of thieves, patrolling every night to steal properties, rape and murder. Security agency forcefully apply law, incarcerate robbers in prisons, but crimes continue daily despite all these efforts. Criminal psychologist has the answers. From psychodynamic theory, originated from the psychological observations by Sigmund Freud (1856-1939), centralise childhood experience as the important factors in understanding why crimes still happened. The theory maintained that, individual personality is controlled by unconscious mental processes that are guarded in early childhood, and id (a primitive part of person that is present at birth), ego and super-ego constitutes human minds. In this regard, due to id, represent biological pleasure provides platform for crimes to achieve that, and also the process at childhood development has crucial effect to one's behaviour. For instance, post-colonial ghetto youth exposed to filthy, criminal-corrupt environment at childhood, whereby fraud cases are not a surprise because this is the environment. A crime such as gender based violence escalates in ghetto areas in critical studies resulted from a couple's childhood background, exposed to such environment. In this regard, the post-colonial ghetto space is more characterised by corruption, violence and high criminal activities which construct the personality of ghetto youth to behave in a criminal way, to meet the demands of id which is biological pleasures. Apart from this, ego and superego goes beyond a criminal control, whereby morality, the consciousness understanding of good and bad is evident. It is argued that, criminal minds is characterised by the underdevelopment of super ego. In this regard, the collapse of Africa's community psychology based on Ubuntu resulted from colonialism and coloniality, is blamed for the existence of crimes in ghetto streets. Manganyi (1974) conceptualise the dialogue relationship of the blacks and world as open lived space favouring white supremacy; clearly explains how Soweto ghettos are haven of crimes, since the most purported culture is supposed to be key to the development of one's super-ego are reduced, relegated to the periphery. Post-colonial ghettos in Zimbabwe are havens of crimes as a result of the collapse of Ubuntu which mends the development of morality in one's consciousness. Gabriel Tard (1843-1904)

Behavioural theory suggests that individuals learn from each other which explain how crimes are committed as learned discourse. In this regard, ghetto as highly populated areas and constituting high crime rate; this criminal behaviour is learned. From instance, the MaShurugwi terrorist activities, are learned by individuals through social contact in mining areas, joining the gang being to terrorise and rob people. Cognitive theory explains the idea of perception and explains how crimes are committed (Jacoby 2004), these criminal intentions or perceptions develops into behaviours, hence crime is committed. In this regard, criminal psychologist explains largely why crimes are committed but based on the mind as the engine of human being, the environment also plays a most important role to crimes since it provides resources for learning, information and blend personality (Schmalleger 2008). The spread of criminal activities in Zimbabwe post-colonial ghettos resulted from the absurd economic environment, which make life meaningless thus suicide as an option but is morally unjustifiable (Camu 1954). Hence the struggle to survive invites criminal ideas. The presence of coloniality unspares ghetto being in crime activities, since Fanon (1967), makes it clear that, the dames, the wretched of the earth stripped off dignity and capable of doing any sorts of crimes as objects better explains Xenophobia in South Africa, as imposed criminal behaviour by the colonial system (Maldonado-Torres 2017, Wynter 2015). The misinterpretations of gender discourses breeds gender based violence, whereby assault cases are reported in highest numbers in Zimbabwean ghettos. Though psychologists argued that it is resultant from the underdevelopment of superego, lived-experience construct personality, but coloniality of social space is also to be blamed. What constitute personality, perceptions and lived experience of ghetto being? Coloniality as a condition and system survived at the end of colonialism is responsible for shaping criminal mind-set, though not to a highest magnitude since some factors such as lived experience and poor governance played a pivotal role. Foucault once blamed the establishment of prisons as power mechanism for social control, the reflection of Africa's past where it survives without prisons for years but less criminal activities resulted in the presence of community values. Foucault (1980) advocates for changing the criminal mind-set by deconstructing the structural criminality through community psychology. Ghetto is not immune to crime but it challenges the liberation project of ghetto cosmology.

Delusional Images; Ghetto Being and Drugs

The escalation of drug abuse among 'ghetto youth' in post-colonial Zimbabwe unfolds as the crisis of national building; it is sort of like a culture that defines 'being a ghetto youth'. It is a sorry case to the future society since toxic drugs circulate in ghetto streets ranging from marijuana, heroin and other dangerous hallucinatory drugs. In most cases, the origin of such behaviour is responding to the continuity of ghetto conditions as a way to escape the realities of post-colonial economic tragedies defined in the lances of political and economic crisis. As a way out as they claim, it accomplishes the continuation of ghetto conditions by the political environment since it compromises the effective application revolutionary objectives towards better political space for youth. A drug creates a serious social disorder. In the context of Jamaican ghetto in 1940s, the society bleeds due to serious drug abuse to escape the unbearable ghetto conditions. In most cases ghetto as a condition are created by the capitalist who saw the opportunity to destabilise the oppressed through selling drugs. It kills thousands of revolutionary souls; continues to fence in oppressed people into ghetto conditions thus drug abuse is a betrayal to revolutionary culture of ghetto cosmology. Jamaican dancehall as European rock music are reported to be drugs induced genre whereby marijuana, cocaine and other drugs are used to stimulate performance. This kind of behaviour obliterates the objective to liberate ghetto being from ghetto condition.

Self-Hatred and Demeaning of Ghetto Being

The problem with ghetto being is self-hatred which resulted from the imposed thinking of inferiority by the creators of that ghetto conditions. Ghetto as a condition continues to show the impacts of coloniality of being since it is formulated in the objective to remove humanness to the oppressed. Maldonado-Torres (2017) made it clear, in South Africa the creation of separatist policy established by the residential designs of two zones, zones of beings and zones of non-being, whereby blacks are referred to as non-beings. The apartheid social structure stripped humanity from the soul of the black folks. The pedagogy of it implemented firstly as cultural toxication, dehumanized and demonized the other.

> "Colonialism denotes a political and economic relation in which the sovereignty of a nation or people rest on the power of the nation, which makes such a nation an empire. Coloniality, on the other hand, refers to long-standing patterns of power relations that emerged as a result of colonialism, but that define culture, labour, intersubjectivity

125

relations and knowledge production well beyond the strict limits of colonial administration. Thus coloniality survives colonialism. It is maintained alive in books, in criteria for academic performance, in cultural patterns, in common sense, in the self-image of peoples, in aspirations of self, and so many other aspects of our modern experience. In a way, as modern subjects we breathe coloniality all the time and every day (Maldonado-Torres 2007; 243)

In this regard, ghetto experiences of self-hate as the manifestation of imposed inferiority complex, rooted in survived coloniality from colonialism. The social structure goes beyond the psychology of the oppressed and maintains the oppressor's ideology as aspects of social realities which are embedded on superior-inferior relations. The creation of ghetto was not just an establishment of a residential area and lived-space condition, but the creation of the inferiors who today needs a serious attention to unlearn the ghetto conditions, unthink the existing 'standards of thoughts' and re-learn in an attempt to restore confidence. It makes sense Steve Biko discovery, in arguing that "the most potent weapons of the coloniser is the mind", whereby ghetto conditions are inserted into the black minds to make them believe black is ugly, black is a curse, black represent devil and colonise even the colour of God, for them to be a superior being in the society (Clarke 1998). Manganyi (1974) argued that blacks conditioned psychologically to think like Soweto is an inferior suburb to Sandton, to think like Mbare is an inferior Suburb to Mount Peasant therefore the highest goal of youth from these ghetto areas was to live in the low density suburb, to be involved in white lived space. In this regard self-hate, self-denigration, disempowerment becomes the mental order of a black being in ghetto. Grosfoguel (2020) warns decolonial scholars to be critically aware of the continuities in discontinuities, whereby the colonial hanger over continue in the so called post-colonial society. Ghetto cosmology need to be Afrocentric, remember the dismembered and restore confidence, existentiality of black bodies, mind and soul towards emancipatory projects in global society.

"The Egyptian Sphinxes and pyramids, the Tunisian city of Carthage and the Great Zimbabwe, the ancient universities of Alexandria of Egypt, Fez of Morocco, the timeless wildlife conservation and ecological skills of the Khoisan people, developing expertise in mining and production of finished products (iron and smelting in Munhumutapa and Mapungubwe) and well organised economies and social political governance as exhibited by the Timbuktu of Mali, Azana of Aksum, Cetshwayo Kampande of Zululand and Tangwena people of Southern Africa, one can surmise that Africa was becoming a great power in the civilisation of the world" (Bhurekeni 2019; 90)

In the process of re-establishing confidence in ghetto being, once stripped of dignity, remembering the past glory remains the trusted methodology, planting the right mind-set towards the glory of a black person. In contemporary ghetto cosmology self-hate manifest in form of imitating the European being, of course cultures are not incomplete, must be merged with other cultures to form a complete axiom, which Santos (2002) call 'diatopical hermeneutic' but the way it justifies the existence of neurotic disorder resultant to coloniality of being. It is resulted from how the past has been dismembered in classrooms and media, but what need to be done is to remember the dismembered (Asante 2007, Broodryk 2002 and Marimba Ani 1994), viewing Africa in its own ontological aesthetics. Manganyi (1974)-transcendental analysis of being-black in the world informed by sociological schema of ghetto conditions, as mental conditions of domestic violence due to misinformed gendered policies, drugs, illiteracy, dump, ugly and vulgarity. This philosophical catharsis differentiates the discourse of Us (blacks) and them (whites) based on racial differences, classes and communication inequality which eventually relegates the blacks to the foot note of social civilisation. Ghetto being is historically produced through colonialism, slavery and coloniality. It further capture the way post-colonial ghetto thinks as inferior beings destined for violence as 'madness' (Fanon 1967). The imaginary constructed creates a shameful culture of vulgar which is alien to African Ubuntu, and demeaning self-hate language which left the revolution incomplete. Ghetto youth in streets are not ashamed to use vulgar language and challenge the objective of ghetto cosmology for being incompatible to the Ubuntu, the virtue of being human. Self-hate as demeaning which Marcus Garvey and notable Pan-Africanist warned the blacks not to practise since it retrogrades the revolutionary culture as is seen in the post-colonial ghettos. Dr Frances Cress Welsing studied black conditions in the USA and found out that the escalation of demeaning language in music is the reason why mental slavery is still a powerful force to the people of the colour, which even transcended to post-colonial Zimbabwe ghetto condition.

"We are the only people on this entire planet who have been taught to sing and praise our demeanment. I'm a bitch. I'm a hoe. I'm a gangster. I'm a thug. I'm a dog. If you can train people to demean and degrade themselves, you oppress them forever. You can even program them to kill themselves and they won't even understand what happened" (Cress Welsing 1991)

This issue is also seen in Zimdancehall music, supposed to be a ghetto renaissance it celebrates self-demise by singing the demeanment language. In this regard, post-colonial ghetto youth in Zimbabwe failed to be immune from the complex coloniality and swim in the pool of self-hate and demeanment which breeds a lot of phobias such as xenophobia in South Africa ghetto, though it is not much of focus of the paper. What makes ghetto culture of the 1950s succeed is the realisation of Ubuntu, but the post-colonial generation ghetto cosmology swept away by modernity and European way of life invested in some senseless quest for freedoms. Harlem Renaissance and Afro-diaspora ghetto culture realised the need to embrace African ethics and the most glorious act to achieve liberation goals. The collective identity of ghetto cosmology compromised by vulgar as an emancipatory project needs to create platforms based on ethical restoration to complete ghetto cosmology liberation agenda.

Conclusion

In nutshell, ghetto conditions breeds serious social pathologies such as prostitution, self-hate, crimes and demeanment. Conceptualising being according to Husserl, Heidegger and Manganyi provides critical epistemology to explain a ghetto being as a construct of environment and consciousness. Coloniality consumes the hopes of the liberation project, whereby ghetto renaissance is about deconstructing the existing confusions identified in identity crisis, sell hatred and criminalism.

Chapter 11
Beyond Ghetto Culture: A Decolonial Project in Post-Humanistic Globe

G hetto is said to be created by European colonization to establish full human exploitation and political control in colonies. The condition relegates the native to the periphery; hence ghetto culture by no means is an incomplete version of liberation projects since it is incomplete in Afrocentric sense. It is the objective of liberation project to remember the dismembered and help Africans sail though into the waters of post-coloniality, in this regard it should be decolonial at the same time Pan African. Why Pan African and decolonial? These questions forms the discussion of this chapter in differentiating Pan Africanism and decoloniality as redemptive philosophies since the former liberates the continent politically and the later focuses on human liberation through epistemic freedom. It aimed at providing a comprehensive thought of political and intellectual emancipation from the snares of the horrific European colonialism and the complex global coloniality. Post-colonial ghetto culture does not just focuses on fighting the political systems but engage in decolonial praxis in post-humanistic world. The methodology of liberation are still Eurocentric, hence a direct call to decoloniality of being, knowledge and power as trusted method to proliferate the human liberation as the goal of post-millennium society

Key Words, Decoloniality, Post-coloniality

Introduction

Can ghetto cosmology be post-colonial? This is a strange question but a vehicle towards a critical understanding of the relationship between culture and the present. It is asking about the existence of ghetto in the supposedly present which is post-colonial. It builds a literary analysis of this paper and constructs arguments to sustain decolonial movement as a liberationist project. The struggle for post-colonial Africa left the continent vulnerable to all sorts of abuses, endogenously and exogenously. Searching post-colonial Africans contents and context of the present Africa is unmatched to post-coloniality. Post-colony remains aspiration (Mbembe 2001) which conceptualise Hannah Arendt theory of emptiness; she asserts that Africa is not yet independent and no longer colonised, describing the emptiness of the situation, that is to say it is difficult to say Africa is in colonial epoch or post-colonial hence the era is unnamed instead described as 'emptiness'. Transcending to ghetto cosmology, though pan African pro-democratic but decolonial project remains unfinished due to the matrix of coloniality whereby Ndhlovu-Gatsheni (2013) call it post-colonial neo-colonised Africa trapped in the snare of Euro-American modernity. This chapter is aimed at fencing ghetto culture in decoloniality, and is divided in various sections explaining the themes of music as decolonial strategy, the question of democratic movement in decolonial borders and decolonial alternatives as humanistic projects to ghetto being, space and cosmology. This paper is informed by post-structuralism Afrocentricity and Transmodenity theoretical propositions.

Imagining Chimurenga Music in Post-Colonial Ghetto: A decolonial Music

Music is a part of society and heals the society; unites the society and influences a certain movement, and communicates ideas, a spiritual act and revolutionary act. Music and society are indispensable, this is confirmed by critical analysis of the antiquity or classical society, dependent on music for spiritual reason, harmony, healing and inciting social values (Chikowero 2008). Ancient empires such as Egypt, Munhumutapa, Persia and Rome history prove that there was a different genre of music used for various purposes, accompanied by musical instruments such as lamellophone, violin, drums and guitars. Music heals the broken hearts, heals the inner soul, communicates sorrows and gives happiness. It is a soul of the ghetto and largely defines ghetto culture. It is not easy to talk of ghetto cosmology without development of music as youth initiatives. From the pre-independence experience, Thomas Mapfumo, Oliver Mutukudzi and other musicians (Chikowero 2013) attracted large followers at the performance in urban areas to heal ghetto broken hearts as caused by brutal colonial oppression. It is now a culture of music to nourish optimistic allusions to the once marginalised society. The struggle for Zimbabwe cannot be written completely without appreciating the role of music, Chinx Chingarira, Jiti music at pungwe and spiritual music all connects the African souls hoping to be unchained and facilitates the zeal to fight for the liberation. In the liberation struggle, the mass mobilisation to the movement was through music, mostly at pungwe, slogans chanted and the revolutionary spirit invoked by music (Matiure 2009, Chikowero 2013, Turino 2008 and Vambe 2012). The all-night gathering and dancing unites the subalterns, provides the spiritual atmosphere of fighting for the same objective and the same people. Mbira (lamellophone), Ngoma (drums), hosho (handshakes) and various instruments, but mostly traditional accompany night singing and dancing (Berliner 1994 and Matiure 2009). This signifies an Afrocentric decolonial version of liberation music in most cases those who are possessed with spirit mediums, possessed and speak to the crowd about the liberation strategy. In this regard music as part of the society is a revolutionary act to embrace the spiritual movement across cultures, it gives assurance and confidence. Spiritual movement is a process whereby a group of people defend a belief, with one accord and revolutionary consciousness. In storytelling, gatherings or before expeditions music is performed; it opens up the gates of spiritual universe to enable the soul to travel far lands, the land of the past (Vambe 2010). What is the use of music in ghetto? What is a decolonial music? Ghetto residents established by the colonial masters as labour reservoir and the situation communicates the message of superior-inferior dichotomy, some music genre such as rock and roll exported to Africa from Europe, but the relationship, between cultural residues in ghetto and pre-colonial past help to establish a post-colonial soul through music, which was once dismembered. A decolonial music premised the confluence of dismembered culture and liberation project, became a popular culture in war of independence, relating to the soul and energises the movement. Decoloniality as now a popular discourse provides a subliminal diagnosis of the contemporary mental confusion caused by colonialism and global coloniality (Mignolo 2013, Ndhlovu-Gatsheni 2013, Maldonado Toress 2018 and Grosfoguel 2019); is based on galvanizing the alloys of unthank Cartesian-Eurocentric canon of thought of "I think therefore I am", in restoring the Afrikology template of thought (Nabudere 2013) informed by African values summaries the following phrase state as "I am because I belong", that is to say knowledge is cosmos not individualistic. Ghetto cosmology through street football and bridge rendezvous, unites the youth and recognises their relevance in relations with public space, music become a cementing factor. The return to the past was through mbira music, internationalised and modernised by Jege A Tapera, Dumisani Maraire, Hope Masike, Chioniso Maraire and other notable mbira groups continuing cultural artefacts of the past like Mbira dzavadzimu, Nyunganyunga and karimba nhare (Matiure 2009). The mixture of technology and mbira creates a new genre titled Afro-jazz invading the ghetto streets; Oliver Mutukudzi and Thomas Mapfumo become more popular. In tracing decolonial music as emancipatory systems in ghetto culture there is need to also question how music can be decolonial? Africans manage to preserve musical heritage, in the sense that post-independence generations though influenced by the existence of western cultural forces, formulated related genres to the past musicography. Not forgetting Zimdancehall, Zimbabwean invention follows the Jamaican dancehall and Harlem Hip Hop style which confirms its commitment to decolonial project. Afro-jazz once popularised by Thomas Mapfumo and Black Spirits, refined by poet-musician Oliver Mutukudzi mixed with South African township music and preserved by poet-musician Mukudzei Mukombe (Jah Prayzah) as Afrocentric version of singing, singing for Africa, by Africans to Africans provides a lasting anointing to the once dead African cultures. This music was not just for entertainment but decolonial intellectual movement whose aim is to deposit decolonial thoughts in contemporary ghetto culture. Besides Afrocentric Jazz music, Jiti music back into scene as not disturbing but a hit entertaining music recreating the images of pre-colonial celebrations, colonial pungwe and the dynamics of new culture. Freddy Manjalimu once popularise it and spread across the ghetto, but Baba Harare came with a stunning contribution to the music.

Remembering Afro-Inclusive modes of Governance: A Decolonial Democracy

From African past, democracy is not alien to Africa, since well governed societies such as Mandinka Kingdom, Ndebele State, Oyo Empire to mention a few use inclusive modes of governance whereby citizen participation were alive to influence decision on juridical cases, war and state of affairs (Diop 1983), hence the need to restore this blueprints must be included in ghetto cosmology. What is a decolonial democracy? How can democracy be decolonial? Struggle to make sense of this contested values work hand in glove with ghetto culture through the objective of liberties and freedoms. Knowledge on democracy is situated to the Euro-American modernity, express western cultures and have nothing to do with values of global south, hence the need of decolonial democracy remembering the past African political blueprints to redefine a true sense of governance and leadership. Ghetto revolution is a voice of the people speaking about democracy in every corner, streets and bridges but do they know what democracy they are talking about? Decolonial democracy is based on Afro-centred human rights, extend it to the virtue of being human and privileges, whereby Fanon (1967) put it logically as the classless society, whereby subalterns or peasants also influence decisions in the political affairs. The contemporary neo-liberal democracy is not about human liberation, but sustaining dehumanisation process originated from the power relations of self (Europe) and the other (global south), hierarchies the relations to create the zones of human being and zone of non-beings. The demonization project developed from Eurocentric anthropology and systematic theology refers Africans as no-thinking beings, people without history, and people without soul and less scientific to the Europoids. All these descriptions disqualifies Africoids humanness, hence their culture is demonized to become dehumanized beings and relegated to the periphery. The process of tribalisation as a European construct problematize the post-colonial political stability since in Darfur Sudan Europeans favour other ethnic groups, give them lands and deprive others which creates a serious hatred, exploding after thirty years of draught and left thousand corpses in Sudan (Mandani 2003). In this regard ghetto situation was about removing the humanness in Africans, creating settlements for labour reservoir with poor living conditions and breed serious phobias, violence and crimes. In search of humanness, ghetto revolution relates to decolonial democracy, focuses on unchaining the minds of urban dwellers. Though its focus is political demonstration against the colonialism in the past and the current political-fascism, but the involvement is to redefine youth as humans, contrary to the past colonial labels which used animalistic discourses as synonym to 'black being', its re-humanization strategy aimed at creating ghetto post-colonial being, demonstrating post-colonial reasoning and image (Mbembe 2003). The re-humanization strategy demonstrated in the contestations of norms, understanding government and European structures of exploitation replacing it with more revolutionary mode of governance, source structural systems from the past as template and refines it for the future. Decolonial democracy solicit redefinition of ghetto being and the discourse epistemic freedom, valuing Afrikology template of the art of knowing (Nabudere 2013). The most astonishing part is ghetto understanding of political values and democratic values defined in neo-liberal approach continue to dehumanize ghetto being as non-thinking object and dismembered the roots of African being. For ghetto being the fight for liberation, the need to unlearn the learned alien values is of urgent Importance; to unlearn neo-liberal democracy, Euro-modernity and lifestyle. The tragedy with African democracy is that it is at the same time Pan African, and the problem with the ideology is that it is an incomplete Afrocentric version. This particular discourse has challenged the post-colonial ghetto cosmology on its commitment to decoloniality as avidly a mental liberation process about re-centering the once denied humanity to claim humanity in demonstrating cognitive competency in global affairs

Ubuntu-ethical values in Humanising Ghetto Cosmology

The cannibalistic nature of ghetto culture, betrays decolonial emancipatory project. Reading from previous articles, ghetto culture is more infested with drug abuses, crimes, self-hate, identity crisis, religious blasphemy, violence and political crisis rooted in ghetto being as colonial construct and proliferated by the contemporary absurd condition. The fortunate part of ghetto culture is its foundation premised on redemption, emancipation and liberation. How can this be humanised? Before relating ghetto culture to the context of humanising, ghetto culture is associated with emancipation, liberation and redemption which made it a complete human centred system. Ghetto cosmology came in response to colonial brutality, racial segregation, labour exploitation, political nihilism, poverty, sulbaternity of youth and poor service delivery due to corrupt bureaucrats. This complex situation, qualifies it as liberationist project centred on human civilization as post-humanistic agenda, though stiff cannibalistic but the human projection rails on the optimistic discourse of freedoms. As explained in the above section, ghetto culture resurrects the dead humanity once murdered by the malevolent colonial system, through intellectual movements replicates Harlem renaissance, political consciousness demonstrates the need to dismantle unorthodox political system and youth development. The reclamation of humanity in the 21st century ghetto, whereby even in ghetto conditions in Soweto, Abuja, Makokoba, Kampala or Nairobi aids the search for decolonial being and search for post-colonial sustainable development. Music came into play to heal the ghetto soul and energise revolution. In Zimbabwe ghetto culture qualified as post-colonial Zvimurenga meaning a series of wars but confined to heritage and the power of cultures. The residue of culture once provides a source of strength of the revolutionary culture. In this regard, the need to humanise is based on the context of deconstructing ghetto being colonial and drug culture and remembers Ubuntu cultural values to materialise revolution.

Conclusion

Ghetto culture is made of people, but where are they coming from? Society, Families and institutions in search of post-colonial Africa play a critical role in shaping the behaviour and thinking of ghetto being through imposed images and social stereotypes. It is pragmatic to decolonize ghetto being, decolonise universities, social systems and to give strength to the most glorious revolution of the 21st century. Ghetto culture has been as the source of any emancipatory activities, but is it possible to achieve that emancipation? Is it achievable? Of course not in fullest context, but the glimpse of freedoms might be evidenced and the decolonial strategy is of utmost importance in ghetto cosmology, being and space. It is a decolonial project in post-humanistic globe, similar to Senghor's theory of Negritude as the preservation of cultural glory, African personality and response to racism in the global space.

Chapter 12 (Conclusion)
Epistle to Ghetto: Post-scriptum thoughts in search of Uhuru naUmoja

The after–thought of this collection of essays is themed on providing the opinions of the author over the prescribed widely discussed subject on ghetto being, space and cosmology in post-imperial Zimbabwe. Ghetto being defined as the reflections of ghetto life sourced from colonial and post-colonial conditions, a confusing and redemptive mentality which relates to the blueprints of the past societies, present and for future better world. The space which comprises of institutions, societies, individuals and experiences shape the modalities, behaviour and the thinking of a ghetto being, however in search of post-colonial Zimbabwe, which has not yet appeared on the map of post-colonial society facilitated by the ghetto being as composed of the peasants, workers, youth and woman who are marginalised and better understand their revolutionary consciousness. That is to say, when the oppressed realised the catastrophe of oppression inhumanity of the conditions revolution become inevitable. Dambudzo Marechera penned House of Hunger, a glorious literature presentation which even is celebrated in his post-humus condition, not only in Zimbabwe but Africa and world at large. The book expresses the ghetto conditions as house of hunger, defined in terms of identity crisis, brutality of colonialism, racism, black existentiality in Diasporas and the post-colonial state crisis. These conditions arguably creates a paranoia, dillusioned, schizophrenic, self-hatred, absurdity and mental slavery, in this kind of the situation those who realise their freedoms incite revolution to reclaim self-images, confidence and full humanity.

In this collection of essays, it is discussed in large sums of literature with convincing justification and presentation of evidence, whereby a ghetto being in post-imperial Zimbabwe is due to availability of revolutionary texts, a revolutionary consciousness cultivated. In Zimbabwe situation the history of ghetto is composed on the middle income class, workers and peasants, peasants are much found on the rural areas but the discourse of ghetto cosmology has no geographical boundaries which demarcates rural and urban, it goes beyond that, so in this regard all classes or groups of people play a most decisive role in the reclamation of humanity and self-image but mostly in a different way depending on the degree of oppressive environment. Fanon (1967) and Ngugi wa Thiongo (1983) highlights the issue of the problematic discourse of liberation as it was hijacked by the petty bourgeoisie, the most alienated and always embrace the European life style. In the novel, Devil on the Cross, Ngugi wa Thiongo made it clear that those who fought for liberation struggle marginalised in post-independence state claimed to represent them, reduced in paupers and beggars and the middle class sell the country again to the former colonisers. The struggle for post-colonial state continue the discourse of class struggle, which should not be the problem today if Africa had listened to Kwame Nkrumah, the petty bourgeoisie are controlling everything and impoverishes the peasants, referred to as ghetto being in this collection of essays. It is believed that the ghetto being revolution is real, will be the real revolution or Cultural Revolution which dismantle all oppressive systems and creates a genuine post-colonial state. The existing ghetto conditions, responded by ghetto cosmology to reclaim the full self-image of the ghetto being continue to create vulnerability to the independent states, in form of proxy wars and neo-colonialism and coloniality, hence this collection of essays is an informative, diagnostic and prescriptive discourse towards the existence of Africa's glory.

Frantz Fanon Post-Colonial Alternatives and Author's Philosophical Convictions

> "The unpreparedness of the educated classes, the lack of practises links between them and the mass of the people, their laziness, and lot to be said their cowardice at the decisive moment of the struggle will give rise to tragic mishaps" (Fanon 1967)

Education is the tool to change the world, Nelson Mandela attest, but what kind of education? Frantz Fanon lambast the educated people as unfit to lead the post-colonial journey since these are the most alienated people, alienated from their cultures as a result of being indoctrinated with Eurocentric superiority. The coloniality of education creates egoistic individualistic removing the true image of self and blind folds the educated with the universalisation of European version of truth, of course these are people led liberation struggle, channelled the most administrative works. Amilcar Cabral also supports their leadership, but it ends up being a Eurocentric model of emancipation which creates social consciousness without reaching national phases, that is the reason the struggle for post-colonial society is still embedded on fighting western imperialism and western oppressive models in African governances.

> "And it is clear that in the colonial countries the peasants alone are revolutionary, for they have nothing to lose and

everything to gain. The starving peasant, outside the class system is the first among the exploited to discover that only violence pays. For him there is no compromise, no possible coming to terms: colonisation and decolonisation is simply a question of relative strength" (Fanon 1967)

Frantz Fanon demonstrates the role of peasants in liberation struggle as the most revolutionary group, confident and spirited to deconstruct oppressive structures through violence, it is absolutely based on the study of decolonial revolutions spearheaded by the peasants as foot soldiers ruthlessly confronting the unjust. Peasants are the most marginalised groups, but not alienated from the society like the educated one, they suffer all the colonial conditions, ghetto conditions and oppressive conditions but the most advantageous to them is presented by Amilcar Cabral on the role of culture as a source of unity in revolutionary act, that is to say as there are relegated to the periphery, they still own some little glimpses of cultures which solidifies them into a formidable revolutionary army. From this perspective ghetto being are the most marginalised group in colonial and post-independence episodes, in this regard there are key strategic groups in the creation of post-colonial Zimbabwe which is not yet there, though political independence was granted, but the individual liberties and freedoms of the soul and mind are still in chains. The ghetto space evidently creates a new form of renaissance, which helps African renaissance to achieve its aims in reclaiming the African lost-self and creates a genuine post-colony. It's an arm to challenge violently the existing social norms based on the complex coloniality and afro-fascist politics through music, literature, poetry and active citizen participation. Frantz Fanon is the most referenced philosopher by the post-colonial writer, a material bank to the theory of post-coloniality, decoloniality and Transmodernity. In this regard, the educated and the peasants, they should not have been a gulf as presented by Fanon, but a collective engagement through decoloniality of epistemology and public spaces.

Epistle to Ghetto: Second Coming of Nehanda

"She has travelled long distances through time to meet this vision for the future: She knows that her own death is inevitable, but sees its significance to the future of her people" (Vera, 1998:11)

The second coming of Nehanda is not in human form, but in spirit as she attest that her bones will rise again to battle the Europeans who stole land of forefathers, her spirits seen in second Chimurenga and never go back since blacks are still in chains, mental and cultural slavery. Ghetto being embraces the spirit of Nehanda, the spirit of fighting in the form of Cultural Revolution as to dismantle the residues of colonialism and the complex coloniality. Ghetto is a marginalised space, but spiritually awake and alive. The conditions are unbearable but the culture is trusted in the creation of a revolutionary society, with the objective to fight all forms of oppression. Ghetto beings are the foot soldiers and trusted revolutionary cadres, the condition is bad the culture is optimistic. As presented in the previous essays, ghetto space and being provides sufficient need in the crusades to facilitate the evangelical mission of decoloniality, anti-dictatorship and anti-neo-colonial gospel, to recruit foot soldiers beyond ghetto geographical location. As hammered by double consciousness, the triple heritage still provides the little ashes to light the fire, a revolution. It is popularly known that good leaders provides good times, and weak leaders provides bad times, but in Zimbabwe only good leaders were from pre-colonial times, the likes of Changamire Dombo, Mizilikazi, and the Munhumutapa, but the collapse of pre-colonial society creates a ceaseless era of bad leadership, from Ian Smith to post-colonial Robert Mugabe and his right hand man Emerson Mnangagwa who assumes power through coup. Of course the post-colonial Mugabe is a celebrated Pan-Africanist, anti-imperialist and revolutionary who challenges the global powers at the international forum and through the land reform programme; his leadership at home was repressive. The hopes of Emerson Mnangagwa to deliver a better economic system, unfolds an era of militarism, serious inflation and continuity of abject poverty as a result of mismanagement of funds, policy inconsistency and sabotage premised on the question of legitimacy. But the idea of engagement was not that bad, open up the nation to the global complex, though a critical failure to diagnose the global coloniality. These two gentlemen, unlike Ian Smith are produced by colonial institutions, inherit them and are alienated to the past. The verdict of their leadership capacity is not the objective of this work, it depends with political commentators which method and yard sticks is used to measure their leadership, the objective of this collection of essays, particularly this epistle is to provide a revolutionary awakening to the ghetto being in search of self-image and remembering the dismembered. Ghetto being is not a coward, is not a drug addict, but a replica of pre-colonial being that respects Ubuntu and demonstrates self-confident through the lenses of Afrocentric view of the society towards the creation of genuine post-colonial society. The platform must be based on the theme of unit, unites all ghetto beings under a revised Ubuntu-ghetto cosmology in search of true meaning of liberation from the ghetto conditions, coloniality and oppressive political system, that is to say searching for uhuru (independence) naUmoja (unity). The discourse of ghetto social consciousness must be at the same national phase to avoid the liberatory miscarriages. The second coming of Nehanda, as already experienced in second Chimurenga, the spirit is also there to inspire another form of revolution, which is cultural revolution from the marginalised people and ghetto being to establish a true sense of post-colonial Zimbabwe. The word Zimbabwe symbolises culture and the past history of the country, which even today narratives try to restore but in the public space it is still at the margins or at deathbed lying unconscious, so ghetto cosmology due to its urban-rural interface profess a cultural revolution to restore the historical glory for present and future political affairs of the country, and continent at large.

References

Adichie, N. C. (2006) Half of the Yellow Sun, New York: Anchor

Adichie, N. (2014) We should All be Feminist, New York: Fourth Estate

Ani, M. (1994) Yurugu: An African-centeredness Critique of European Cultural Thought and Behaviour, New York: Africa World Press

Anzaldua, G. (1987) Borderlands/La Frontera: New Mestiza, Aunt Flute Publishers

Asante, M. K. (1995) Afrocentricity: The theory of Social Change, Philadelphia: Temple University Press

Asante, M. K. (2007) An Afrocentric Manifesto, Philadelphia: Temple University Press

Berliner, P. (1994) The Soul of Mbira: Music and Traditions of the Soul of the Shona People, Chicago: Chicago University Press

Bhebhe, N. (1989) Benjamin Burombo: African Politics in Zimbabwe 1947-1958, Harare: College Press

Broodryk, J. (2002) Ubuntu: Life Lessons from Africa, Pretoria: Ubuntu School of Philosophy

Butler, J. (2004) Undoing Gender, London: Routledge

Butler, J. (2012) Subjects of Desire: Hegelian Reflection in Twentieth-Century France: Columbia

Cabral, A. (1969) Revolution in Guinea: An African People's Struggle, New York: Monthly Review Press

Caputo, J. D. (1996) Deconstruction in a nutshell: A conversation with Jacques Derrida (Perspectives in Continental Philosophy), Fordham University Press

Chigora, P. Mahomva, R.R and Lunga, M. Eds (2019) Reinventions and Contestations of Thought-Power in Africa: Emerging Perspectives on Pan Africanism, Bulawayo: Leaders of Africa Network

Chikerema, A.F. (2013) Local Democracy and Citizen Participation in Zimbabwe

Chikowero, M. (2008) Struggles Over Culture: Zimbabwe Music and Power 1930-2000, PhD Thesis, Dalhouse University

Clarke, H.J. (1993) Who Betrayed Africa and other speeches, Trenton: Third World Press

Clarke, H.J. (1993) Harlem Voices from the Soul of Black America, New York: E World Inc.

Clarke, H. J. (1998) My Life in Search of Africa, Trenton: Third World Press

Connell, R. (2012) Transsexual Woman and Feminist Thought: Towards New Understanding and New Politics, Journal of Feminism

Cress Welsing, F. (1991) The Isis Papers, Key to Colors, Third World Press

Daimon, A. (2007) Migrant Chewa Identities and their Constitution through Gule Wamkulu? Nyau Dance in Zimbabwe, African Union Conference Centre, Society, State and Identity in African History 4th Congress of the Association of African History

Daimon, A. (2008) "MaBhurandaya": The Malawian Diaspora in Zimbabwe, 1895 to 2008, PhD Thesis University of Free Sate

Daimon, A. (2018) Totemless Aliens: The Historical Antecedents of the Anti-Malawian Discourse in Zimbabwe, 1920-1979, Journal of Southern African Zimbabwe, volume 44

Derrida, D. (1973) Margins of Philosophy, Chicago: University of Chicago Press

Diop, C. A. (1974) Origins of Africa Civilisation, Myth or Reality, New York; Presence Africaine

Dussel, E. (1980) Philosophy of Liberation, Duke University Press

Fanon, F. (1967) The Wrecthed of the Earth, Paris: Penguin

Foucault, M. N (1969) The Archaeology of Knowledge and the Discourse on Language, Paris: Edition Gallimard

Gaidzanwa, R. (2000) The Images of Woman in African Literature, Harare: University of Zimbabwe Press

Gilroy, P. (1993) The Black Atlantic: Modernity and Double Consciousness, New York: Harvard University Press

Grosfoguel, R. (2007) "The Epistemic Decolonial Turn: Beyond Political Economy Paradigms, Journal of Cultural Studies, volume 21 (2/3), pp203-246

Heidegger, M. (2008) Being and Time, Haper Perennial Modern Classics (Reprint)

Hudson-Weems, C. (2004) Africana Womanism: Reclaiming Ourselves, Beldfed Publishers

Kapuya, Z. (2019) Phenomenology of Decolonizing the University: Essays of Contemporary Thoughts in Afrikology, Chitungwiza: Mwanaka Media Publishing

Kingsley, M. (2019) A Music Genre Crows in Zimbabwe, Fuelled by Rage Against Authority

Kufakurinani, W and Mwatwara, W. (2017) Zimdancehall and the Peace Crisis in Zimbabwe, African Conflicts and Peace Building Review, volume 7(1) pp 33-50

Lezra, E. (2014) The Colonial Art of Demonizing the Other, London: Routledge

Lugones, M. (2003) Pilgrimage/Peregrinates: Theorizing Coalition against Multiple Oppressions (Feminist Constructions), Rowman and Littlefield Publishers

Machingambi, I. (2007) A Guide to Labour Law in Zimbabwe, Harare: Machingambi Publications

Machingura, F. (2011) The significance of glossolalia in the Apostolic Faith Mission, Zimbabwe;
Studies in World Christianity 17(1): 12-28.

Mahomva, R.R. (2014) Pan Africanism from Cradle, Present and Future, Bulawayo; Leaders of Africa Network

Mahomva, R. R and Moyo, S. (2015) Post-1980 Chimurenga Explained, Bulawayo: Leaders of Africa Network

Makumbe, J. (2009) Zimbabwe a Survival Nation, Harare: University of Zimbabwe Press

Maldonado-Torres, N. (2007) On the Coloniality of Being, Cultural Studies, volume 21 (2) pp 240-270

Maldonado-Torres, N. (2014) "Thinking Through the Decolonial Turn: Post-Continental Interventions in Theory, Philosophy, and Critique-An Introduction, Transmodenity: Journal of Peripheral Cultural Production of Luso-Hispanic World, Volume 1(2)

Mandani, M. (1996) Citizen and Subject; Contemporary Africa and the Legacy of Late Colonialism, Princeton, NJ: Princeton University Press

Manganyi, C. (1974) Being Black in the World, Pretoria: Wits University Press

Matiure, P. (2009) The Zezuru Mbira Dzavadzimu and the Legacy of Spiritual Possession: The Efficacy of Mbira Dzavadzimu within the Zezuru Cosmology Berlin; Lampert Academic Publishing

Mazama, A. (2003) The Afrocentric Paradigm, Trenton: Africa World Press

Maxwell, D. (1999) Historicizing Christian independency: The southern African Pentecostal Movements 1908-1960. Journal of African History 39(2): 243-264.

Maxwell, D. (2002) Christianity without frontiers: Shona missionaries and transnational Pentecostalism in Africa. In Christianity and the African imagination: Essays in honour of Adrian Hastings. Edited by D. Maxwell and I. Lawrie, 295-332. Leiden: Brill.

Maxwell, D. (2006) African gifts of the spirit: Pentecostalism and the rise of a Zimbabwean Transnational religious movement. Harare: Weaver Press.

Mazrui, A. (1986) The Africans: A Triple Heritage, London; BBC Publications

Mignolo, W. D. (2013) The Darker Side of Western Modernity, Duke University Press

Mudimbe, V.Y. (1988) The Invention of Africa: Gnosis, Philosophy and Order of Knowledge. Indiana University Press

Mudimbe, V.Y. (1994) The Idea of Africa, Indianapolis: Indiana University Press

Mugovera, G. Recording Studio in the Ghetto: The Patriot, 4 October 2018

Nabudere, D. W. (2013) Afrikology, Philosophy, Wholeness. An Epistemology, Institute of South Africa

Ndhlovu-Gatsheni, S.J. (2009) Do 'Zimbabwe' Exist? Trajectories of Nationalism, National Identity Formation and Crisis in a Post-colonial State, Oxford: Peter Lang

Ndhlovu-Gatsheni, S.J. (2013) Coloniality of Power in Post-colonial Africa: Myth or Reality of Decolonization, Dakar: Codeseria

Quinjano, A. (2000) Coloniality of Power, Eurocentrism and Latin America, Durham North: Duke University Press

Raftopolous, B and Sachikonye, L. (2001) Striking Back: The Labour Movement and the Post-Colonial State in Zimbabwe 1900-2001, Harare: Weaver Press

Raftopolous, B. (2004) Nation, Race and History in Zimbabwean Politics, In B, Raftopolous and T, Savage (Eds), Zimbabwe injustice and political reconciliation, Cape Town: Institute of Reconciliation and Justice

Raftopolous, B and Mlambo, A. Eds (2009) Becoming Zimbabwe: A History from the pre-colonial period to 2008, Harare: Weaver Press

Ramose, M. (1999) African philosophy through Ubuntu, Harare: Mond Books

Ranger, T. (1985) Peasant Consciousness and the Guerrilla War in Zimbabwe, Harare: Zimbabwe Publishing House

Ranger, T. (2004) 'Nationalist6 Historiography, Patriotic History and the History of the Nation: The struggle over the Past in Zimbabwe, Journal of Southern African Studies, volume 30 (2)215-234

Rodney, W. (1972) How Europe Underdeveloped Africa, Washington D.C: Howard University Press

Sachikonye, L. (1997) Structural Adjustment and Democratization in Zimbabwe, Social Movement in Development: Springer Journals

Sachikonye, L. (2011) When a State turns on its Citizens: 60 years Of Institutionalised Violence in Zimbabwe, Harare; Weaver Press

Sachikonye, L. (2012) Zimbabwe's Lost Decade, Politics, Development and Society, Harare: Weaver Press

Said, E. (20030 Orientalism, London: Penguin

Samkange, S, J, T. (1980) Hunhuism or Ubuntuism: A Zimbabwe Indigenous Political Philosophy, London: Graham Publications

Santos, B. S. (2012) Public Sphere and Epistemologies of the South. African Development, volume XXXVII (1), pp43-67

Satre, J. P. (1993) Being and Nothingness, Washington DC: Washington Square Press

Shivji, I. G. (2009) Where is Uhuru? Reflections on the Struggle for Democracy in Africa, Pambazuka Press

Tivenga, R. D. (2019) Contemporary Zimbabwean Popular Music in the Context of Adversities, letter volume 55(1)

Tendi, B. (2010) How intellectuals made History in Zimbabwe, African Research Institutes Counterpoints

Togarasei, L. (2005) Modern Pentecostalism as an urban phenomenon: The case of the Family of God Church in Zimbabwe. *Exchange: Journal of Missiological and Ecumenical Research* 35(4): 349-375.

Togarasei, L. (2010) Churches for the Rich? Pentecostalism and elitism, In *Faith in the city: The role and place of religion in Harare*, Edited by L. Togarasei and E. Chitando, 19-40. Uppsala: Swedish Science Press

Turino, T. (2008) Nationalists, Cosmopolitanists and Popular Music in Zimbabwe, Chicago: University of Chicago Press

Vambe, M. (2012) Rethinking the notion of Chimurenga in the Context of Political Change in Zimbabwe, Journal of Music Research, volume 8(2) 1-28

Vera, Y. (1998) Nehanda, Harare: Mawenzi House

Wa Thiongo, N. (1980) Devil on the Cross, London: Penguin

Wa Thiongo, N (2007) Wizar4d of the Crow, New York: Anchor

Wiredu, K. (2002) Companion of African Philosophy, London: Blackwell Publishers

Woodson, G. (1933) The Miseducation of the Negroes, African American Books

Wynter, S. (2015) On being Human as Praxis, Duke University Press

Zvobgo, C.J.M. (1996) A history of Christian missions in Zimbabwe. Gweru: Mambo Press

Mmap Nonfiction and Academic books

If you have enjoyed **Not Yet Post-Colonial: Essays on Ghetto Being, Cosmology and Space in Post-Imperial Zimbabwe,** consider these other fine *Nonfiction and Academic* books from **Mwanaka Media and Publishing:**

Cultural Hybridity and Fixity by Andrew Nyongesa
Tintinnabulation of Literary Theory by Andrew Nyongesa
South Africa and United Nations Peacekeeping Offensive Operations by Antonio Garcia
A Case of Love and Hate by Chenjerai Mhondera
A Cat and Mouse Affair by Bruno Shora
The Scholarship Girl by Abigail George
The Gods Sleep Through It All by Wonder Guchu
PHENOMENOLOGY OF DECOLONIZING THE UNIVERSITY: Essays in the Contemporary Thoughts of Afrikology by Zvikomborero Kapuya
Africanization and Americanization Anthology Volume 1, Searching for Interracial, Interstitial, Intersectional and Interstates Meeting Spaces, Africa Vs North America by Tendai R Mwanaka
Africa, UK and Ireland: Writing Politics and Knowledge Production Vol 1 by Tendai R Mwanaka
Writing Language, Culture and Development, Africa Vs Asia Vol 1 by Tendai R Mwanaka, Wanjohi wa Makokha and Upal Deb
Zimbolicious: An Anthology of Zimbabwean Literature and Arts, Vol 3 by Tendai Mwanaka
Drawing Without Licence by Tendai R Mwanaka
Writing Grandmothers/ Escribiendo sobre nuestras raíces: Africa Vs Latin America Vol 2 by Tendai R Mwanaka and Felix Rodriguez

Nationalism: (Mis)Understanding   Donald Trump's Capitalism, Racism, Global Politics, International Trade and Media Wars, Africa Vs North America Vol 2 by Tendai R Mwanaka
It Is Not About Me: Diaries 2010-2011by Tendai Rinos Mwanaka
Chitungwiza Mushamukuru: An Anthology from Zimbabwe's Biggest Ghetto Town by Tendai Rinos Mwanaka
The Day and the Dweller: A Study of the Emerald Tablets by Jonathan Thompson
Zimbolicious Anthology Vol 4: An Anthology of Zimbabwean Literature and Arts by Tendai Rinos Mwanaka and Jabulani Mzinyathi

Soon to be released

Writing Robotics, Africa Vs Asia, Vol 2 by Tendai Rinos Mwanaka
Zimbolicious Anthology Vol 5: An Anthology of Zimbabwean Literature and Arts by Tendai R. Mwanaka and Tembi Charles

https://facebook.com/MwanakaMediaAndPublishing/

www.ingramcontent.com/pod-product-compliance
Lightning Source LLC
Chambersburg PA
CBHW030334270326
41926CB00010B/1626